C000260748

FATHER STONOR'S LOVE

Father Stonor's Love

Letters and Sermons
OF
Dom Julian Stonor, O.S.B.

Preface *by Peter Kreeft*
Foreword *by Nonie Drexel*
Introduction *by Dom Julian Stead, O.S.B.*
Afterword *by James P. MacGuire*

Angelico Press

First published in the USA
by Angelico Press 2022
Copyright © Angelico Press 2022

All rights reserved:
No part of this book may be reproduced or transmitted,
in any form or by any means, without permission

For information, address:
Angelico Press, Ltd.
169 Monitor St.
Brooklyn, NY 11222
www.angelicopress.com

paper 978-1-62138-893-7
cloth 978-1-62138-894-4

Book and cover design
by Michael Schrauzer

And that freedom of ours—to ignore him, to give him an occasional grudging smile or, like Mary, to want to spend all our lives at his feet in complete surrender to his love—is our most stupendous privilege, given to us alone of all the visible creatures that God has made. And it is also a tremendous personal responsibility resting on each one of us, for each one of us is completely unique in the history of the world and like a separate creation. We, and we only, can give God the love of our particular heart. And in the whole eternity for which each one of us has been irrevocably created there is only this one brief period of our earthbound life during which God is watching to catch those fleeting little looks of love which he knows cost us an effort but which represent our real free spontaneous love.

Father Julian Stonor, O. S. B.
Sermon: "The Children for Whom
the Nursery is Adorned"

CONTENTS

PREFACE

by Peter Kreeft

I am now in my eighties, and there are a fairly large number of readers who, through the seventy-plus books I have published, know me well enough to ask me to read their unpublished manuscripts and, if I like them, to write introductions or at least blurbs for them. I estimate that these submissions now number about thirty a year. About fifty percent of them I reject (politely, I hope) without more than a fairly cursory browsing because it is quickly evident to me either that they are embarrassingly badly written or that I am embarrassingly incompetent to judge their specialty. About another forty percent I read a little more conscientiously and then write polite but sincere letters to their authors saying that I claim my privilege of being a curmudgeon and therefore I demur from recommending manuscripts that do not make me know, understand, appreciate, or enjoy something I did not know, understand, appreciate, or enjoy before, even though they may very well be publishable and will probably do a significant quantity of readers a significant quantity of good, either religiously, morally, affectively, or cognitively. That leaves about ten percent that I enjoy reading and therefore happily write introductions for (or, more often, just blurbs). Far fewer than one percent, or one every three or four years, I see as a treasure, a discovery, and a gem of which I want to sing the praises to the whole world. (This singing, like all singing, is one of the many works of charity that are also great fun!) This is one of them.

What the reader will meet here is not merely a "what" but a "who." Father Stonor may well be canonized one day as a saint, but even if not, he is certainly a *mensch*: beautiful, delightful, intelligent, loving, erudite, and eloquent—the consummate gentleman. To meet him in these pages is a rare delight.

I was made aware of this holy, priestly gentleman by another such holy, priestly gentleman, Father Julian Stead (also O. S. B.), whom I knew through Sheldon Vanauken and Tom Howard, and who reminds me of still another gentlemanly and holy English priest, Father Walter Hooper. (If you know and love any one of these four holy gentlemen, I guarantee you will love Father Stonor.)

I use the word "gentleman" with great care and even awe, since the species is nearly extinct. A gentleman never forces himself on you. But Father Stead so uncharacteristically enthused about his discovery and admiration of Father Stonor's writings (gentlemen do not usually "enthuse"!) that I promised to examine them, more for his sake than for my own. When his middleman Dr Tim Flanigan sent me no less than five volumes of his writings, I was not enthusiastic but a bit intimidated. I anticipated a fairly quick browse-through, enough to satisfy my classifying them into one of the usual categories, thus honestly but minimally fulfilling my promise to read them.

Instead, I was hooked.

What I found here is one of the rarest things in the world, in both senses of the word "rare": intrinsically precious and very hard to find. There is a sanctity and humanity here that I can only call hobbit-like: humble, ordinary, totally human, earthy, unspectacular, and obviously the fruit of many years of cultivation. It is what I found remarkable in my brief meetings with the two people we know are saints, Dorothy Day and Mother Teresa of Calcutta. I call it "extraordinary ordinariness." Anyone who would not want a man like Father Stonor as his priest, his grandfather, his uncle, or his biological father simply does not know what a good man is. Father Stonor is a man who stands at the exact opposite extreme from the verbal pyrotechnics of a Nietzsche, with his sudden bursts of brilliant, attention-demanding, Germanic thunderings and fist-pumpings, screamings and spittings. Father Stonor is literally a gentleman—and alas, in our age we have forgotten that real manliness is gentle and true gentility is manly. (We have also forgotten the strength of truly feminine femininity, unless we have retained a personal devotion to the Blessed Mother.)

The kind of man you meet in Father Stonor's letters to Noreen is a vanishing breed, and if we do not cultivate that breed again our civilization is doomed to be conquered by the barbarians who now dominate our media. I see seven qualities of such a man in these letters, and if you have never met such a man I plead with you to read this book through at some time when you are at leisure and at peace. I say "at leisure" because its charms are like the tide rather than like a storm or a crashing wave: they creep up on you, and when they do they are irresistible.

First of all, they are personal gifts, written by hand. Today few people are even capable of legible penmanship, and even if they are, they are too hurried and hassled to take the time for this personal gift. Instead, they turn to their robot slaves to do their work for them. Our slaves today are made of metal and computer chips, not flesh and blood, but we have the same dependence on them as slave masters have always had on their slaves.

Second, they are letters, not tweets or posts or instagrams. They use the King's English, not a bastard mixture of symbolic logic, rap, and vowelless codes. They are elegant. They dress for dinner. They take time. They help us to enact one of the most radical and universal revolutions possible: they reverse our slavery to time. They make time serve them rather than making themselves the slaves of time. (Why does no one notice the supreme irony that technology, which is essentially a series of efficient time-saving devices, has robbed us of leisure? Where did we put all the time we saved? Into caring for our slaves.) We learn this art, this revolution, as we learn morality: not by abstract precept or the will to try it but only by imitation of concrete examples. Here is an effective example and model to imitate.

Third, we find in these letters what the Greeks called *storge*: homeyness, *Heimlichkeit*—including *Gemütlichkeit*—familiarity, intimacy. It is the humblest kind of love. Is there any word we love and long for more than the word "home"? (Remember how that one word tugged at your heart and your tears when you heard it from E. T.?) Heaven would not be heaven if it were not our home.

Fourth, we find genuine human friendship (*philia*), which the Greeks considered the very highest form of love. They would gag at our notion that a "friend" is merely one of thousands of anonymous names on Facebook. A friend is a special, unique, precious, and irreplaceable individual.

Fifth, we find the specifically and radically Christian kind of love, *agape*, which mirrors the love of Christ, who mirrors the love of God, the very life of the eternal Trinity.

Sixth, we find a deep priestly desire (*eros*) on the part of Father Stonor for God and for Noreen's union with God in dozens of little ways, most of them hidden. Father Stonor mediates Christ's love to Noreen because that is the very essence of a priest.

Finally, we find a refreshing absence of sexual *eros*. In our time of multiple disclosures of sexual predators, even priests, here is an example of the Saint-Francis-and-Saint-Clare relationship, of what the Greek Orthodox Akathist Hymn to the Theotokos calls "tenderness conquering desire." Noreen is definitely a feminine woman, and Father Stonor is definitely a masculine man, and we see many of the simple but forgotten dimensions of the rich and subtle God-invented gender differences in this relationship.

And we get all that from just the personal letters. Father Stonor's homilies are incomparably richer.

I grew up in the Dutch Reformed Church (Calvinist-Presbyterian tradition), and was used to long doctrinal sermons that were often quite theologically profound, in fact formidable, though very long. Since there was no Mass in Protestant services, the sermon was the center of Sunday worship. When I became a Catholic, I discovered that Catholics do not preach sermons but give "homilies." This was an improvement in two ways: as their name suggests, homilies were more "homely" or homey, and also they were mercifully short. However, they were also usually pretty slapdash and banal. They compared with Protestant sermons as a quick splash in a tide pool compared with a trip in a submarine into the ocean depths.

Well, the homilies of Father Stonor are to the old Protestant sermons what the sermons are to ordinary parish homilies. They are what the great old hymns of Isaac Watts or John Wesley are to those embarrassingly happy-sappy little "praise choruses" that are so inexplicably loved by all Baptists. They are what Catholic cathedrals are to modern "mega-churches" that look like rock concert halls or high school auditoriums. They are elegant; they are prose that verges on poetry; they are *literature*. Like Gothic cathedrals, they appear to be works of art that took a long, long time to make, with great thoughtfulness and loving care. They are seriously holy. And they are contagious: they move the reader or listener to love holiness. Read them aloud: they sound as if they came from visiting angels rather than from recently-evolved apes.

They often refer to the Last Judgment, the next world, and our ecstatic heavenly destiny, as seamlessly and naturally as if Father Stonor is already living there and here at the same time. Like many of the saints and like Christ himself, Father Stonor speaks of our otherworldly destiny that "eye has not seen, ear has not heard, nor has it entered into the heart of man" side by side with a vivid awareness and love of the concrete little things of this world, both natural (such as its birds and flowers) and human (such as the details of Noreen's ordinary life). Both worlds evoke in him (and in us by a "good infection") a joy that is natural, spontaneous, and habitual, not an imposed and remembered religious duty. We find it increasingly difficult, in our culture of diversions and distractions, to be both serious and joyful at the same time; Father Stonor shows us what C. S. Lewis meant when he wrote that "joy is the serious business of Heaven."

His interpretative retelling of Biblical narratives, from both the Old Testament and New, are elegant without being elitist, thoughtful without being abstract, full of fresh insights without being clever and verging on heresies, and simple without being simplistic. They are what homilies were designed to be. Even if we have heard these stories many times, our interest is piqued because we know Father Stonor will put new, beautiful music to the old words.

I am one of thousands of readers who will be thanking God for inspiring these gems and also thanking Father Julian Stead and Dr Tim Flanigan for rescuing these treasures from the forgotten mines of the past.

FOREWORD

by Nonie Drexel
a.k.a. Pussywillow

I hope I will be able to add a family perspective to these remarks on Father Julian Stonor. I think it is important to recognize that this collection of letters represents just one window onto a fascinating life, and I very much hope that one day a full biography may be written.

I wish I could properly describe what it is like to grow up in a family where faith is just an ordinary part of life. Like good health, it is taken for granted, and likewise it often weakens and fails. My parents as well as my cousin Father Julian Stonor came from families where it was a normal condition to wax and wane in faith as well as in health, to question everything, to dream and doubt and wonder, to try to intellectualize one's feelings or just simply to feel them, and even in the loss of faith, to be able to recognize moments of grace.

These letters tell part of a family history, one of a generation that precedes mine, one which was largely defined by World War II, but also one where faith was always part of the story.

Cousin Julian, as he was known to us, embodied something that can only be described as true holiness. He was totally human and of this world but you did not need to be a Catholic or even a believer to sense the spirit that moved within him and through him to touch others.

It was during the post-war years that Father Julian and my mother, Noreen Stonor Drexel, became life-long friends. I will try to give some context for my mother's experience. Born in 1922 to a recusant family, she grew up in a very sheltered Chiltern valley, obsessed with horses, barely educated, and entirely unworldly.

I can't even begin to detail the history of Stonor where she grew up—indeed Cousin Julian was the foremost expert on that—but it remains to this day the home of one of the oldest Catholic families in Britain.

Before the outbreak of the war, my American-born grandmother moved part of the family back to Newport, Rhode Island, for their own safety. My mother suffered terrible home-sickness throughout the war, and felt a keen sense of having deserted the cause. She trained as a Red Cross nurse and ambulance driver.

She and my father travelled back to Britain in the immediate post-war months to visit the family there, and the earliest letters in this collection are dated from this time period.

My parents, siblings, and cousins all remember from their youngest days that Cousin Julian was someone with whom you could discuss anything. He might not have had an answer, but he would not be judgmental, or disdainful, or horrified, and would always know how to respond, often with a story or an allusion to history which always made one think and try hard to seek out the meaning. He seems to have made deep connections with many people using his special balance of empathy and erudition.

No doubt Julian's success in attracting hundreds of new parishioners to Saint Mary's in Liverpool, just like his sympathy with my mother, was rooted in the ability to converse freely and unreservedly. I have a hard time understanding how any of that generation managed to make sense of the war and its aftermath, but I do know that my English family have always been surprisingly free of the stereotypical British stoicism. As a tribe, we rarely refuse to examine emotions. This ability to delve and probe and discuss did not, however, often result in the kind of emotional and spiritual bond that developed between Cousin Julian and my mother—that seems to have been quite unique.

Cousin Julian had endured the unutterable horror of war and clearly suffered a resulting crisis of soul, mind, and body. His letters allude to what appears to have been a nervous breakdown by 1946. "Shattered" is the word that reverberates. He clearly had suffered unspeakable trauma during the war, and one has to ask how it was possible for him to continue to give spiritual strength to others when his own was in tatters. It is indeed a painful exercise to try to imagine what he saw and heard and endured, as well as to remember that the attitudes of his generation were far less attuned to this kind of psychological trauma. He was on the beaches during the Battle of Boulogne, and a history of his regiment, the Irish Guards, gives the following description of the evacuation. Perhaps there may somewhere exist a far more in-depth description of Julian Stonor's war experiences, but to me what this glorified militaristic account both does and does not reveal, is absolutely heart-rending:

[T]he Germans were closing fast and the perimeter shrinking ominously. In this situation of imminent danger the Battalion Padre, Fr Julian Stonor, embarked on his personal crusade. Running from slit trench to slit trench he gave everyone absolution. As he later wrote, "any number, and not all of them Catholics, told me that from that moment afterwards they felt no fear." Pressed from all sides and under fire from Germans now dominating the high ground overlooking the harbor, the remains of the two battalions re-embarked again on HMS Whitshed.

Up the Micks: An Illustrated History of
the Irish Guards, by James Wilson

Then we have Julian's letter of August 30, 1947 referring to my mother's first arrival at Boulogne as another link between them—I know from many conversations with my mother that she and Julian did indeed discuss his wartime experiences in some depth. In this letter Julian refers to "Hugh's diary" and I am certain this means an account of the war which was written by Hugh Dormer (d. 1944), an officer of the Irish Guards and also an English Catholic educated at Ampleforth. He was a close friend of Cousin Julian and shared many traumatic experiences on the front in France. Dormer writes in his diary "Certain people like Julian Stonor are intended as beacons to the world, reminding men of the eternal existence of those high ideals which call men out against all reason and self-interest...." The sense of purpose that both Hugh Dormer and Julian strove to find in the war effort, and which Julian shared with my mother, was deeply rooted in a love of nature and "the unique mellowness and richness of the English countryside." Dormer describes a conversation with Cousin Julian in which they agreed "men must be reminded of the extraordinary nature of the everyday world...the wonders and beauty of the spirit..." (Hugh Dormer's Diary, April 22, 1944). This sense of wonder and connectedness to the natural world is something my mother felt very deeply, and is certainly what she and Julian communicated during all their conversations while sitting up on the Warren, the hill behind Stonor.

Sad to say, my mother's letters to Cousin Julian are not part of this collection, which may seem an enormous omission and certainly requires some explanation beyond the fact that most of them have been lost.

Noreen Stonor Drexel, in spite of being the adored child of an aristocratic family, never attended school and to her own agonizing shame, was barely literate. Although a great reader and a truly sensitive intellect, she could hardly write—in today's terms, probably not beyond fourth grade level. But write to Cousin Julian she certainly did, confiding her deepest doubts and worries, the depressive tendencies which seem to have afflicted the whole family, as well as the joys which she sometimes struggled to share with those closest to her. My father often failed to understand her fully, and he and I (as well as others in the family) had a disgraceful habit of putting her down intellectually. "Insufferably sincere" is one cruel phrase which I remember. The fact that she sent Cousin Julian her scrawled and misspelled letters is to me an extraordinary testament to her trust in him, and to her certainty that she would be safely heard and understood, rather than judged by him. And it gave her a huge sense of confidence in herself that he could mutually confide in her.

She often struggled to find a sense of purpose, and felt torn between her husband and her children. My father loved to travel and was bored by domesticity; the issues for their marriage were always city versus country, New York sophistication versus the old dream of that sheltered Chiltern valley. For my mother Cousin Julian was a link to her childhood, her place of origin, her faith, and her soul.

They bonded over horses too, which to today's reader might sound a quaint and privileged sort of hobby. I believe though that for Julian especially it was a way to heal the shattered nerves of war. The other great bond seems to have been over the children, their achievements, their school, their teeth. Cousin Julian was fully immersed in the family lives of both Drexels and Stonors even while he was living in distant parishes in the north of England. I am continually enchanted by how the letters convey a sense of daily life and news of friends within such a loving and spiritual framework.

Maybe the reader cannot pick up on the subtle ways in which Julian influenced and even corrected my mother; his chiding is so gentle that his guiding hand becomes just an organic part of their conversation. Without detailing the family dynamics, one can discern some sense of tension between my mother and her sister-in-law Jeanne Camoys. That tension certainly existed, but it would be very incorrect to demonize my aunt and uncle who did a great deal to shelter and support a huge number of stray relatives at Stonor, Cousin Julian included. They had inherited an indebted estate which they felt deeply obliged to maintain. It's also important to remember what post-war Britain, even for the landed gentry, was really like. Austerity and rationing continued into the 1950s. Sherman's and Jeanne's children, my first cousins, were born into an economy where the occasional bantam egg was a great treat. I believe they had appalling medical and dental care in their youth, perhaps even vitamin deficiencies, by comparison with their spoiled American cousins. Children of the kindly West, we drank fresh-squeezed orange juice every day. My parents used to travel to England with an extra suitcase filled with toilet roll, Kleenex, and other American staples—the British equivalent being either not available or not soft enough. The disparity between the two countries was huge, and not just in terms of luxuries. Reading between the lines I can hear Cousin Julian very gently directing my mother's attention and conscience toward a better understanding of differing family perspectives, without ever quite reminding her of what advantages she might be taking for granted. Meanwhile, Julian himself was living in some of the most disadvantaged parts of Britain, and working tirelessly, often in very impoverished environments, and to the detriment of his own health.

I myself barely remember Cousin Julian; for me he was a figure in the folklore of our family. As a child one could ask a difficult question, like "what did the Holy Spirit do before the coming of Christ?" and my mother would look into the distance and reply, "Cousin Julian could discuss that with you." My siblings and first cousins of course knew him very well. What always struck me most in their stories about him was a sense of fun and mischief and magic. My mother said that he shared Tolkien's and Lewis's ability to fascinate children with history and stories. Even adults noticed his way of magically appearing and disappearing in the house, like a creature from Middle-earth. He certainly recognized and celebrated the aura around Stonor itself, and in no way discounted the idea that our pagan predecessors took part in the spirituality that the place has always inspired.

I very much hope that Father Julian's esprit comes through in this collection of letters, even for readers unfamiliar with all the people and places and events. To his close family as well as to so many others, Julian was an extraordinary figure: a truly holy man, yet a vibrant participant within the family, a living breathing example of the intersection between the spiritual life and the day-to-day. He gave to all of us children a view of life infused with a sense of mystery and of hope, of merriment too, and ultimately of sanctity.

INTRODUCTION

by Dom Julian Stead, O.S.B.

BACKGROUND

Father Stonor, a priest of the Order of Saint Benedict's English Congregation, died, aged fifty-two, on February 12, 1963. Men and women who choose to live a monastic life in the Order of Saint Benedict, do not join the Order as such, but one of the monasteries belonging to it. They take a vow of "stability," lifelong obedience to the abbots elected by the one autonomous monastery. An Abbey may set up a "Priory," a community governed through a Prior the Abbot appoints. There may also be "missions," parishes subject to the Abbot's jurisdiction, with a monk or two as pastors. A monk priest can also be assigned to an Abbey of nuns as chaplain in residence. Father Stonor found himself in assignments of each sort.

Father Stonor, when still eighteen-year-old Robert Stonor, chose to join Downside Abbey, where he had been at school from age eight. In 1933 Downside moved its preparatory school (boys aged eight to thirteen) to Crawley, Sussex, as Worth Priory. In 1934, as a junior monk still doing his theological studies for the priesthood, Stonor was sent to Worth as guest-master in the monastery and to teach in the school. He was ordained a priest at Worth on the Feast of Christ the King in 1936.

During World War II he served as a chaplain to the Irish Guards. Having served at Worth Priory for years before and after the war, he was appointed to missions in Somerset, Cumbria, and Liverpool. Devoutly attached to the Celtic monks of the early Middle Ages, he was delighted to spend his last days in their land, North Wales, at Talacre Abbey.

Another locality to which he was devoted is Stonor Park, the residence of his family from deep in the Middle Ages. For his gallantry at the battle of Agincourt its squire was awarded a hereditary peerage, as Lord Camoys. They were a recusant family during the centuries when Protestantism was imposed as the state religion. Men and women found guilty of disobeying the law by fidelity to the Catholic Church were subject to capital punishment; many are honored as saints in the Catholic Church, with the title of "martyrs"; quite a few were connected with the Stonor family as members, or used the Stonor estate as a hideout. Thomas More is the best-known of the saints from whom Father Stonor was descended. Some Jesuit martyrs were housed at Stonor; Saint Edmund Campion operated a printing press in a tunnel beneath the hill above which has stood the family's dwelling since the twelfth century. Father Stonor wrote a history of the locality and his family in *Stonor*, published by R. H. Johns Limited in 1951. This is one of the few places in England where the Catholic Eucharist has been celebrated without a break for so many centuries. The atmosphere defies description.

NOREEN STONOR DREXEL

Father Stonor's favorite cousin was Noreen Stonor, about eleven years his junior, born at Stonor Park; her mother was American. Her family moved to America before World War II, and she married John Drexel. She and her husband passed away in Newport, Rhode Island, early in the first years of the twenty-first century.

Administrators of her estate found among her effects letters from "Cousin Julian"—set apart perhaps because she liked to reread them. They were very private, intimate revelations of the author's soul, such as may pass between close friends or religious persons and their director, and definitely not intended for public consumption. Knowing of my close friendship with Father Stonor, these administrators drew my attention to these letters. The family had, in fact, asked me to be on the look-out for sources of use to a biography of Father Stonor. When the administrators sent the letters to me to read, I was astounded. I saw that they would be a valuable addition to English spiritual literature.

Their author almost seems to have seen God and heaven with his own eyes, which affected the way he saw his fellow man and the rest of creation. His approach to his mission placed less emphasis on holy fear and contrition (both good and necessary, to be sure), and greater emphasis on seeing souls with God's eyes. Perhaps Father Stoner's vision of Goodness itself was the key to his genius for bringing out the good in us. The good is what he saw.

LETTERS
1947–50

Carmelite Convent, Exmouth
30 August 1947

Dearest Noreen,

Your lovely letter waiting for me here on the 28th did more than anything to restore my shattered nerve. Because my horizon now is no longer bounded by the next conference of the retreat, but by the knowledge that I will be seeing you again on the 12th when it is all over. A picnic lunch would indeed be lovely and I will write to Lady Wentworth today to ask if we may see the Arabs [horses].

I am so glad you had such a lovely crossing, and that your first glimpse of France was Boulogne Harbor from the bridge of a ship. I feel that is another link binding us together. I have managed to get you a copy of Hugh's diary, as I know you two would have loved one another so much, but I don't know what the rules are about sending books to France, so if it is forbidden I will send it to your hotel at Folkestone.

With my love to you both. And thank you ever so much for such a sweet letter, especially when you were feeling sick and can't have felt like writing. Now that I have known you and that you are away I can understand <u>exactly</u> what your mother must feel! Bless you always—

Julian

WORTH PRIORY
CRAWLEY
SUSSEX

OCT.16.1947.

Dearest Noreen,

Today I have been promoted to pen and ink instead of scribbling in pencil, as I am sitting up for an hour, so I want my first proper letter to be to you, though not knowing yet whether you have started for California I must get Sherman to forward it.

I can't tell you how much I loved your letter and shamefully got each of the different nurses to read it to me as though it had only just arrived! And, as you can imagine, I was touched to the core by your dear kind Johnny coming all the way to Worth again to see me on your last day, when you must have been so desperately busy packing and he was already so tired by the journey from France.

I had heard from the nurses that the weather was being rough during your crossing, so I am so glad you weren't sick. You certainly put me to shame, as during those four or five days I couldn't swallow even a spoonful of tea without being sick, which I am told was merely a nervous reaction to the pain, so I am feeling very humiliated. Actually the thing seems to have taken a firm grip on me, because although the eye opened at last on October 11th it is very bloodshot and I still have to lie in the dark without any visitors except the Prior. At least the privacy enables me to keep my self-respect because I am afraid there are still periods when I can only clutch my eye while the rest of me wriggles like an eel!

Sherman has perhaps told you that, apart from its being, I hope, good for me in itself, it has brought about a great change in my fortunes, as when I am better I am going to Downside permanently, which is what I have always longed to do since the age of eight (and I am now nearly forty!) and to what I think is the nicest post there, as secretary to the Abbot, whom more and more people are beginning to venerate as a real saint.

Well, that is more than enough about me and, what with day-dreaming, I see my hour is nearly up. I do want you to know as a fact, Noreen, that I wouldn't have missed my last chance of seeing you and Johnny even if I had known that I was going to get shingles for three years, though of course my most vivid memories of you will always be in the park at Stonor, and especially that evening up at the Warren. I do hope it won't be too long before we meet again, as, though I usually hate talking, I still feel I want to talk to <u>you</u> for days on end—meanwhile I am sure you will love every minute in California, and, above all, with so many unhappy marriages everywhere, it is such a wonderful comfort to know that you are absolutely secure in the care of someone who really does seem to be kindness and generosity personified.

With my fondest love to you both and, of course, many more than daily thoughts and prayers—

always your affectionate
Julian

Downside Abbey
14 Dec. 1947

Dearest Noreen,

I had indeed been longing for your letter as you guessed, though I was always able to console myself by reading your last one!

I do hope you both have a lovely Christmas, with at least a <u>few</u> days alone together, with Pamela and Nicky. But I can imagine how difficult it must be to refuse any of the invitations to the constant parties without hurting people, because, just <u>because</u> you are so inadequate, as you call it (though that is not the word <u>I</u> would have chosen!), and because Johnny too is so absolutely natural and unspoilt, you must both be like a breath of fresh air at those sophisticated parties and you would be <u>really</u> missed if you didn't go, whereas I expect half the other people wouldn't be at all.

But the thing that thrilled me most in your letter is that there is even a chance that you may be coming to England again next summer. This time you must bring a nice pair of old jodhpurs and we will get some horses from somewhere, so that you can show me all the lovely bits of the Stonor country that I haven't seen, and I will show you the places where some of the more exciting things in the family story happened.

Incidentally, while I have been convalescing here I have been able to add lots and lots more to the book and also rewrite the parts which were a bit heavy and sticky, so even from that point of view the illness has been well worth it. It only bothers me now in the evenings and at night; in the mornings and afternoons I would hardly know I had it. I am not allowed out yet, but it is so much better that I am hoping to be able to go to Stonor fairly soon after Christmas.

Please forgive my most unorthodox Christmas card—the snow is the only right part of it—but the idea behind it really is that you should send me in return a snapshot of you and Johnny that I could keep in my breviary. Not being very photogenic, it is literally the only one I have of myself—one of the boys took it at Worth last winter—but if you have plenty of spare ones I would love one too of you with one of the ponies, looking nice and Celtic!

6

With my fondest love to you both and a big blessing on you and on the children, and please give my love and good wishes to your father and mother—and a special lump of sugar to Charmaine![1]

always your affectionate

Julian

---

1 Charmaine is the name of a horse.

Downside Abbey
29.1.48

Dearest Noreen,

I have just spent a lovely fortnight at Stonor, where there was great rejoicing at the news of Johnny's unexpected visit, and where everyone is longing for the summer, when you will be coming too with the children. I <u>must</u> somehow manage a holiday during that time, and it will be my first meeting with your mother, whom I am sure I will love.

Mrs. Cannon's birthday was a tremendous success. She was in wonderful form, and almost all her 137 living descendants came to see her, including 60 great-grandchildren and five great-great-grandchildren. To my amazement she recognized me straight away, and, brushing aside the Mayor of Henley, who was asking very pompously: "To what do you attribute your great age?", asked me if my shingles were better and did I remember when that darling child, Miss Noreen, and her husband took her to Pishill in the car. She had wanted to die after celebrating the day and getting the King's telegram,[2] but now that she knows you are coming again in the summer and bringing the children, she has postponed her death until after then. She held her reception in Mrs. Sears's cottage opposite, where there was hardly room to move all day, and for half an hour I got completely wedged between old Mrs. Hunt and somebody who thought I was P. J. Hall! (Incidentally the latter is now married and living in Henley.)

The new vicar's coat has far more food stains on it than Father Segres's, to Jeanne's delight!

Perry came over for my last night, which was awfully nice of him, and the Pipers,[3] whom I like more and more, came over several times. I hear he has an exhibition on in New York.

While I was there we took away all the hedges round the front lawn, leaving only the iron railings, and the effect is simply wonderful, and will be even nicer when the deer come down there

2 It is a custom in England that every citizen celebrating a hundredth birthday receives a congratulatory letter or telegram from the King.
3 John Piper, a well-known British landscape artist, was a friend of the Stonor family.

in the summer. And now that the fir trees have gone and the ivy on the chapel, the latter looks unbelievably lovely from right down the drive.

Cousin Julie was looking wonderfully well, and so thrilled that you were coming. And you will be glad to hear that Jeanne paid a surprise call on Francis in London, who has since been telling everybody how charming Sherman and Jeanne are.

Sherman was of course his usual generous self, overwhelming me with kindness, but he wasn't looking at all well, so I do hope the journey to America with Johnny (who does him more good than anybody in the world, by keeping him happy and laughing) will make a big difference to him.

With all my love, Noreen, and <u>longing</u> to see you—

Your affectionate,

Julian

Downside Abbey
16 April 1948

Dearest Noreen,

Whenever I feel tired and depressed I read your lovely long letter written between Christmas and Johnny's return from Paris. And then that starts me daydreaming about your visit this summer and I feel better. Could you please let me know, as soon as it is fixed, what months you will be in England, so that I may make my holiday coincide, as we have to plan ours some way in advance so that too many people won't be away together.

I do want to make the most of every single moment of your visit, because (though, please don't break it to Sherman or Jeanne until I have talked to you) I am pretty sure this will be the last time I will see any of you.

I am still hoping that we will be able to ride together somehow (though I am sure your new jodhpurs will put me to shame!), though I don't quite know how or where, as I would so love to have a picture of you on a horse, as I have always imagined you, to keep in my memory—preferably somewhere nice and wild and windswept like the cliffs of Cornwall, as there are no horses within miles of Stonor. Will you be going down to St Ives again? Because perhaps we could spend a few days there before I come to Stonor, as I can easily get to Cornwall from here, and then I could talk over with you whether or not to break my news to Sherman.

I am so thrilled at the thought that I am going to be able to see your two children too, as I know how much I will love them.

I do hope your dear, kind Johnny doesn't still feel rather conscience-stricken about his relief over his grandmother's departure from this life. Poor thing, she had got so blinded and bewildered and twisted up in her attitude to this life and even to her own family, that for that reason alone one can only rejoice at her having gone into the radiant sunshine of God's love, where she will see everything in true perspective, and where we hope she will have found that most of her blind spots and difficulties of character were not so much deliberate yieldings to selfishness as inherited twists in her character which were more in the nature of a cross which she had to carry, and from which she will now be freed for ever and ever and will be as radiant and fresh and as full of love as if she were a new creation. She certainly wouldn't want to come back for a million worlds, so I am sure she won't want Johnny to be wishing she could!

I did so love all that you wrote about your own missing Johnny while he was away. May your love for each other always grow deeper and deeper, as I am sure it will.

I am afraid I have never been able to do another thing about getting the book published, although it is quite finished; because I am now guestmaster as well as secretary and—to give you an idea of what that involves—we have had 220 guests staying here in the last 30 days (I have to keep a register for the rationing authorities) besides innumerable visitors for the day to be shown round; so that I never get a moment to myself to write my own letters or get the book packed off, except in the middle of the night, if the shingles wakes me up, and then I have to give the letters priority.

With my fondest love to you all and absolutely longing to see you—

always yours most affectionately,
Julian

Cistercian Abbey
Caldey Island
Tenby
S. Wales
Ascension Day, 1948

My dearest Noreen,

You really are an absolute darling—and Johnny too—to carry your generosity to such unbelievable lengths as to offer to pay such enormous expenses and even to forego your own visit to England, for which you were all longing. It is now more than 24 hours since I had your letter and I still have a lump in my throat which nearly chokes me.

I ought really to be very ashamed of myself, because I see now that my thoughtless words were bound to cause you anxiety, and yet I can't be sorry because I know that God saw the love and generosity which immediately welled up in your heart and also the beautiful and humble words in which you clothed your request in order to make it easier for me to accept, and so I know that in the day of judgement He will repay you for that letter and for the love in your heart with a love which mine can never hope to emulate—though I honestly think that not even Johnny could possibly love you more deeply than I do. I have long ceased to regard you as a cousin, but as a darling twin sister, with whom, more than anybody else, I long to share every single ray of happiness and love which God pours into my own soul.

I can only write a short letter now as I don't think I can send more than two pages by air mail, but, before anything else, I want to explain—what, of course, you could not possibly have guessed—that I was not thinking of physical death, though the effect will be the same, but I wrote because I have obtained all the necessary permissions to become a Trappist monk this summer.

In fact I am writing this letter looking out across the Atlantic from the cliff of the little tiny island on which the monastery is situated, as I have been living the life on probation for a week.

I will be returning to Downside on Saturday, but the sad thing is that—as a final test to see whether my health will stand it—the Abbot wants me to return here (for good) <u>as soon as the summer</u>

holidays start, in order to help with the harvest, and so instead of the two or three weeks I was hoping to spend in a last visit to Stonor, I will now probably only be able to see you for a few hours.

Once I have returned here it will, of course, be like dying as far as this life is concerned—no visits or even letters from outside, and on the island perpetual silence so that it won't even affect me that all the other monks—only 12 of them—are Belgian or French. The life is, of course, much stricter than Downside; we get up at 1.30 or 2 and spend till 9.30 in prayer (mostly sung, but some of it private prayer in silence), then there is work on the farm till 11.30, when there is half an hour's prayer till the first and main meal of the day at 12 (only bread and vegetables, but as much as one wants). Then, after two hours' silent reading or prayer, there is three hours' more work on the farm till Vespers at 6.30. At 7.15 there is supper (the same as the midday meal, only smaller), followed by half an hour's public reading and the last sung prayers of the day before going to bed at 9. And there is also more poverty than Downside, as there are no private rooms (we lie down, fully dressed, under a blanket in a common dormitory) and no possessions of any sort, not even a prayer book. But, although it may sound rather grim, in practice it is the most heavenly life; the other 12 are real saints and the setting is so unbelievably lovely that one cannot forget God's love for a single moment. Above all there is the joy of being allowed to obey His call to leave everything for Him, and the knowledge that "unless the grain of wheat die, itself remaineth alone", but that if it die it can really bear fruit and really win God's grace for others, which we can never do by mere human efforts or 'charm'. I will try to write a longer letter when I get back to Downside, because I am counting so much on your understanding. With my fondest love to you both and gratitude too deep for words,

from Julian

Downside Abbey
25 May 1948

My dearest Noreen,

Although I feel sure that Saint Anthony won't be able to resist you any more than I could, for the time being I can only think in terms of your almost unbelievable loss, and the sweet way you have taken it—grieving mostly because of the love (Johnny's above all) which made those jewels far more precious to you than their great beauty and value did. I expect that is why God allowed them to be taken from you (if only for a time), just as He allowed you to think—through my thoughtlessness—that I was going to die or go blind, because He knew how generous your response would be. But please don't grieve to feel that you may have lost those lovely tokens of their love, because their love itself you can never lose. And though with so many people the loss would be so serious because they have to depend to some extent on such things to make them look their best, in your case I am sure no one ever noticed the jewels, however lovely they were.

Now that you are coming so soon, and also because I find it so impossible to get a moment to myself for private letter-writing (it has already taken me two days to write this much), I would rather wait till I see you to explain everything about Caldey, as I realized in my last letter how utterly false an impression I must be giving you. I was wondering whether you and Johnny could possibly come and stay in the guesthouse here for a night before you go to Paris (in case I get whisked off before you come back). I think you would absolutely love Downside, and there is a lovely peaceful garden here where we could talk. Any day except Sunday, June 27th would be all right for me, but if you could manage Tuesday, June 29th (Sts Peter & Paul), you would see the services in the Abbey at their very best and the singing that day would be lovely (there are 400 boys in the school), while, as it is a whole holiday, I would have the whole day to talk to you.

I have just been away for a week, giving a retreat to the girls of a big convent school near here. There were some really lovely children among them, many of them daughters of my Irish Guards officers or sisters of boys here, and as one of the latter—a girl of

18 and a real Celt from Cornwall—had implored me to talk to them a bit, as I had done to her brother, about the things which I loved most, I suddenly thought I would write out the whole retreat as though I was talking to you, and later make a fair copy of my notes and give it to you for you to remember me by, so that you can imagine how moved I was when I got back and found your letter waiting for me to read your request for that very thing.

With my fondest love, Noreen, and longing to see you both—and I hope the children too at Stonor later in the summer.

Julian

Downside Abbey
19 June 1948

Dearest Noreen,

For three days I have been thinking of you getting nearer and nearer, and I am sure everyone must be wondering why I am suddenly looking so radiantly happy!

Provisionally I have booked a double-room in the guest house for the nights of Monday 28th and Tuesday 29th, because I thought there would be an awful feeling of rush and being pressed for time if you left Stonor early on Tuesday morning, because the High Mass starts at 9.30, and it is after that that I am hoping we will be able to have a really lovely uninterrupted talk. I am presuming that you will not be bringing Pam or Nicky here, because I am almost sure that I will be able after all to see them at Stonor in August (but not sure enough to risk it in the case of you and Johnny). There is a real chance that I may be able to spend the first fortnight of August at Stonor, give Tommy and Georgina their First Communion on Sunday the 15th, and then go straight from there to Caldey.

It seems <u>almost</u> too good to be true, but if it is—and I hope I will know by the time you come here, you <u>must</u> be there then, so that we can climb the Warren again, and we might even be able to go for a ride through the beech woods on two of the horses from that place on the Fair Mile.

God has always spoilt me so incredibly ever since I can remember that I think He might easily have prepared this for me too, as my last supreme treat before I go, because He knows that there is nothing in the whole wide world which would bring me a joy which I could even <u>compare</u> with spending my last fortnight at Stonor, with <u>you</u> there and Johnny and <u>all</u> the children together. It makes my heart almost stop to think of it! and with the prospect of being actually sitting with you on the Warren in a few weeks' time, basking in the sun and with that wonderful feeling of peace and security which the park at Stonor gives—as though life could go on like that for <u>ever</u>—it seems almost needless to try and express my thoughts in a letter.

As a preparation for Caldey I have been getting rid of my few possessions (barely enough to fill a suitcase!) and thinking, as I did so, about your really wonderful detachment, which, with all the things that Johnny and others have lavished upon you, has kept you as fresh and unspoiled in your knowledge of what are the most precious things of all as if you were a bare-footed colleen born in one of those tiny white-washed cabins on the coast of Connemara. I cannot think of anyone but you and Johnny who could have suffered your recent loss without becoming embittered and unable to think of anything else, and in your last two letters you haven't even mentioned it, as though it was (as indeed it is in God's sight) only the loss of some lovely shells you had picked up on the beach.

In the course of my destruction I have managed to find these three photos—though still nothing showing very much of my habit, I am afraid!—but at least the one of me as a monk, which was taken only six weeks ago (when I wasn't looking), will reassure you about the shingles, because the last scars have almost disappeared from my forehead above the <u>right</u> eye, which was where I had it.

I am so glad I have found one too of my beloved 'Spanish State', though I am afraid he is looking rather thin there and hadn't got back the wonderful golden sheen on his chestnut coat, while the Shetland, cutting out his legs, prevents you taking in his great height. But you will see how unjustly he had been libelled as an unrideable man-killer, because for weeks I only had that halter and no saddle.

The only other thing I seem to have, which I would like to give <u>you</u>, is a book I wrote during the war—but never published. You wrote that you found the Bible so hard to understand (as indeed it is, for it is a whole <u>library</u> of books, written in quite different languages and centuries and civilizations during nearly 2,000 years, and all bound together with no explanations and in a hopelessly muddling order), and this book of mine—it is only 80 pages—is an attempt to trace the one single story of God's love running throughout and illustrate it with just the loveliest passages, which one can read again and again, leaving out the rest. If I had had time, I would have made it simpler and shorter, but even so I think you will find it a lighter bedside book than the whole unexplained Bible, and at the same time I hope it will remind you to whisper a prayer for me before you fall asleep.

I won't write any more now, as I hope I will be seeing you so very soon. If you do have to ring up, there will be more chance of getting hold of me, if you could make it between

10.00–12.30 AM,[4]

2.00–7.00 PM,

or 8.00–8.30 PM.

At other times there will be services going on in the church, so that you would only be able to leave a message for me.

I know there is no need for me to try to tell either of you how much I am longing to see you again—and also for my first glimpse of Pamela and Nicky,

with my fondest love—

Julian

P. S. Sherman has found out—from the Ascot Convent—about my future; so I am trusting you more than ever to help him understand.

---

4   That is, 10:00 AM–12:30 PM.

Downside Abbey
1 July 1948

Darling Noreen,

Although everything has worked out so differently to what I had planned, I do want you to know that you couldn't possibly have stored my memory with more lovely pictures of you to take with me to Caldey.

It was all so lovely and peaceful and free from tension. In fact I feel as if I might almost have been an invisible spirit watching, unseen, your innermost family life—Johnny, as usual, disguising his unlimited kindness and generosity behind his so loveable mask of lazy good-nature, and yet all the time thinking out—with most exquisite tact—how he can give people the most happiness. (I always think he has just that bigness of character which Baroness Orczy tried to give the Scarlet Pimpernel in her famous novels; and of all the people I know he is the only one whom I would have entrusted you to, if I had been God! Of anyone else I would feel wildly jealous and quite sure that they didn't really love you and guard you nearly securely enough.)

Then there was your darling Pamela, the perfect image of natural unspoilt childhood. The picture of her which I know I am never going to lose as long as I live was of her dancing off with all the utterly unselfconscious grace of childhood to pick dandelions, with that lovely view as the background to the picture and she herself silhouetted on the top of the hill with the wind from the Atlantic blowing her hair and herself unable to keep still for a moment from sheer joy of life, just like a young lamb or a foal. I hope you didn't really mind the flowers which we picked—to wither and die before the day was over. Because, although—like you—I usually hate picking them, they were only <u>made</u> to give us pleasure, and I am sure that in God's sight no dandelions ever fulfilled their purpose more perfectly than the ones whose gold caught Pamela's eye and which He saw being made into golden chains by her fingers. And I am sure He was never so glad that He had given the wild carnations their heavenly scent as when her adorable six-year-old heart felt sorry for that poor little bunch drooping in the car—but only after having fulfilled their Master's

19

wishes more perfectly than all the millions of carnations which were <u>not</u> found and loved by any of his children.

And finally, of course, there was <u>you</u>, who seemed so near this time that even sitting with you again on the Warren couldn't have brought me any greater happiness to treasure. In any case nothing can ever dim my original memory of you there, whereas on a second occasion we might have felt more self-conscious than we did then, and there would have been an undercurrent of sadness at knowing that it was the last time; whereas now my memories of you there and of seeing you as a mother with your child yesterday are both of unclouded happiness, without any tinge of sadness in them; so that they will always seem like a foretaste of heaven.

Even our never having had our ride together doesn't really make me feel any twinge of disappointment, because I can so <u>easily</u> imagine what it would have been like, whether at Stonor or on the hills above Wells. And the presence of that sweet person, Miss Lehman (?), who also shares that love of horses and who kept reminding me of them and of how lovely it is to ride <u>even in spirit</u> over those hills, might have been sent on purpose to make my cup of happiness complete. Incidentally, I am sure it was partly due to her, with her natural freshness and vitality, that I, for one, found the day so absolutely perfect. I had half been dreading it, thinking that all the time I would be conscious of the coming parting (for, although I am sure that that kind Johnny will bring you to Caldey to see me, yesterday was the real goodbye as far as ordinary human family-life is concerned, with its day-dreams of future holidays at Stonor or in Cornwall together and of hours spent with you in some future home like Turville or Bosmore). But her nice happy personality, so engrossed in the happiness of each passing moment, had something infectious about it, so that it was impossible to feel sad and sentimental, and it was only after you had actually gone that I realized fully again how much I will always have to be grateful to her for.

I mustn't make this letter too long, but I do just want to tell you how deep a joy it is to me that <u>you</u> have got my photograph album, which contains the only reminders—outside my thoughts—of all the lovely people and places and things with which God has surrounded me from my earliest years, and which He has now given me the supreme grace to leave in order to be with Him alone. I would never have thought myself to suggest your having it, as it would have seemed like forcing myself upon you, but I was hoping so desperately that you would ask for it! And it was the same with the little crucifix, which I would like Pamela to have one day, but which I would, of course, infinitely prefer <u>you</u> to have until then.

But could you, please, before you go back to America, return me my mother's letters about my father; because I would like to give my sister, Joan, something to remember me by, especially now that she must feel so cut off from the family, and when you have read them I am sure you will agree that they will bring back to her all that is meant by a father's and mother's love and perhaps help her to see what a sad thing she has done by leaving her own children motherless.

Lots of the other things which I would have loved to talk to <u>you</u> about you will find in the book about Stonor and, still more, in the other book which I will send you as soon as it is typed.

With my fondest love to you all and thank you a thousand times for giving me two such heavenly days —

with my biggest blessing —
Julian

P. S. I am enclosing some postcards for Miss Lehman's collection.

Downside Abbey
7 October 1948

Dearest Noreen,

For nearly three weeks I have been waiting until today to write to you, because the first Thursday of every month is a sort of holiday and my best chance for writing letters, so you can imagine my joy when at breakfast this morning I found a lovely long letter from you.

You say very sweetly that I always write just what you want to hear, and this time I really think I will, because my chief news is that after a few heavenly weeks on Caldey (which coincided with the corn harvest and also the most lovely weather, so that the golden-brown fields of corn were bordered by a sea of Mediterranean blue), the Abbot decided that he could not let me transfer after all and that I must accept it as his final verdict that God wants me to remain at Downside.

He couldn't have been kinder about it; nor could the Prior of Caldey, who came back to Downside with me to discuss the question with the Abbot, and of course the joy of knowing for certain what God wants me to do far outweighs the occasional pangs of disappointment when I remember the life on Caldey.

And now that I know that God doesn't want me to give up Stonor and all that it means to me, I have, of course, immediately started looking forward to lovely summers there, with you and Johnny installed in Turville Grange and some friend of yours with a lovely stable-full of ponies at Bosmore—one for each of the seven children—so that you will be able to spend whole days teaching them to ride as well as you and to get to know every path and corner of Stonor.

About the book—I am afraid there has been rather a disappointment, as Burns & Oates (the chief Catholic publishers over here) say that they cannot take the risk of publishing it without a subsidy, as the present cost of books over here is so fantastic that a book like that would cost too much for them to gamble on lots of people buying it. Personally I think it _would_ sell, because I have a list of 60 or 70 people who have read it in typescript and they were enthusiastic about it and put themselves down for a copy whatever the cost. But if your father thinks it would be possible to get it published in America (I think a story of such unequalled antiquity and continuity <u>would</u> appeal to a great number of Americans—especially, of course, Catholics, universities, convents, etc.), I am perfectly willing and I don't suppose there is such a paper shortage with you. I expect there are some firms that have an English branch.

<u>You</u> are, of course, the person whom I am most longing to read it, because you love Stonor so much and I know you will love some of the Stonors in the past just as much as I do, but I would much rather you waited till it is in print, when you can read it properly and in comfort. And the same is, of course, true about the Retreat.

That too is why I am so longing for the day when you will have your own home at Stonor, to which you can escape for the whole summer from the social whirl which you describe, and be your real self among children and ponies and all the scents and sights of the beechwoods and the fields.

I am so sorry about the darling puppy—though what a heavenly one its short life must have been. I am sure it packed more enjoyment into it than most other dogs do in twelve years.

With my warmest love and greetings to Johnny and Pamela, and, as always, a heartfelt blessing on you all (which contains, as God knows so well, my most heartfelt prayer of all—that He will bring you all to Stonor in His own good time) and of course to you yourself a love that belongs to you alone as a sort of twin-sister,

always your affectionate
Julian

Downside Abbey
9 Dec. 1948

Dearest Noreen,

A very, very happy Christmas to you both and to that dear Pamela of yours.

I have found it much easier to settle down after Caldey than I thought I was going to, and one most unexpected thing which has made a tremendous difference is that for the last two months I have had an absolute dream of a horse to school every afternoon for a boy of 17, who is going to be given him for Christmas as a hunter.

He is a big black gelding, 16.2h.h., with tremendous power. He had won several Point-to-Points and Jumping Competitions when he was first ridden—he is now 10 years old—but was very badly broken and whenever he got muddled was given a hiding with a stick, and for the last three or four years was permanently out at grass and running wild. The boy to whom he has been given found it took two hours to catch him and that even then he couldn't do anything with him, and was going to get rid of him, until somebody from Worth suggested my trying to do something with him first. Luckily he had a most lovely sensitive mouth and was only frightened of human beings, not vicious, and has now become an absolute pet. I have never once had to use even my heel on him, let alone a stick. And, to crown my joy yesterday, the Mendip Hunt met only a mile away and the day was a whole holiday! The going was very heavy, but the weather was heavenly, and in a wonderful 75 minutes without a check, mostly over low stone walls, he and a horse ridden by a girl who was whipping-in were the only two who were able to keep up.

I think the chief resolution I came back with is that you simply must take Turville when Aunt Julie dies, and take Pamela and Nicky hunting with you! I am sure there can't be anything else in the world that can give quite such ecstatic joy. And those heavenly lawns and trees would be the most perfect setting for you and Johnny to give hospitality to all your friends. You simply must persuade Johnny to do it.

Sherman is at last taking the chapel in hand. He has had the windows repaired, and is laying a stone floor, and has also had the cupola on the Tower re-painted by dear old West and George Shurfield, who even climbed up and mended the weather-vane.

I do hope you are coming over this summer—with <u>both</u> the children—and for a really proper stay to make up for all the disappointments of last summer. I am sure one long summer, with all the children there together, really getting to know the Park and all the woods round about (perhaps I could borrow some of the ponies from Worth)—would make Sherman forget all his cares, because he is at his very best when he is being the paternal host and trying to give other people happiness. At present all his friends are much older than him and so he can't really play that part properly, but with a house full of <u>young</u> people I am sure he would become his real self.

With my fondest love to Johnny and the children—and, of course, to your father and mother when you see them—as I expect you will—on Christmas Day, and do, <u>please</u>, come over this summer. I can still remember every minute of your visit last year, but of course it had the cloud of my departure to Caldey over it, besides having to be so short, and then there were the illnesses and your having to go to Paris; but this time I am sure we could make it one long foretaste of heaven.

With all my love—
Julian

Downside Abbey
22.1.49

Dearest Noreen,

Thank you so much for your lovely Christmas letter—and especially for the part about which you apologized for just "rambling
on"—I have read that part again and again and again!

As you have so sweetly suggested it, I think I would like the
photograph album back, if you can remember to bring it with you,
as it has almost all my memories of the past locked in it. But the
crucifix I would like you to keep, until you bequeath it to Pam,
because, as you know, I have nothing that I will ever be able to
give you except a few tiny things of sentimental value, and that
was really the chief of them.

I am already beginning to feel thrilled now that the days are
getting longer and there are only four or five months before you
are over here again, <u>please</u> God. Now that I am not teaching in
the school (I am still guestmaster and Abbot's secretary), I think
the Abbot would let me go away in termtime if necessary, so that
as soon as your own plans are more or less definite I will start
pressing to be allowed to have my holiday while you are at Stonor.

I somehow feel sure that everything is going to be perfect this
year, and far more than make up for all the disappointments of
last year. I do hope you are going to bring Nicky as well as Pamela.

I hope you won't mind, but I have given your address to a
monk from here (quite my favourite in the whole monastery)
who has just gone out to our monastery in Washington for six
months. He is going to be giving retreats, in different places, but
hopes to be staying at Portsmouth Priory for some of the time
and, as he expected to be very homesick for England, I promised
I would give him an introduction to you. I am sure you will like
him awfully, he is a bit younger than me, Cornish, and was adored
by the small boys at Worth. His name is Father Victor Farwell.

Incidentally, the Prior of Portsmouth, Father Gregory, is also a
friend of mine and writes me most affectionate letters every few
months, though we haven't met for at least fifteen years!

The horse is still here—looking wonderfully fit now—and as
the owner is asking £500 for him, I hope he will be here always,

as no one has offered more than £350. Perhaps he will let me bring him with me to Stonor in the summer!

We have had a lovely mild winter here so far—the birds have never stopped singing. I hope it has been the same with you.

With my fondest love to you all four and a very big blessing

from your affectionate
Julian

Downside Abbey
2 July 1949

My dearest Noreen,

I am sure you can guess how I am <u>longing</u> to see you both. However busy I have been with guests and visitors, since your letter came, the thought of your coming visit has been with me all the time, even when talking to people.

About dates—of course, you must do what suits you best. As you have been so tired and as the weather is still so hot, it might be best for you to come out from London straightaway. From my point of view there is really no difference between one week and another—the weekends are always <u>very</u> busy, and the middle of the week less so. The Abbot is giving me a fortnight's holiday this year, but, alas, it has to be in August, after you have gone.

I don't remember the name of the hotel in Bath where you stayed last time, but in the course of the year I have discovered that the one which people seem to like best is the 'Francis'.

With my fondest love to you both, and hoping so much that the long journey from Switzerland in the heat won't have undone the effect of your rest.

Always your affectionate—Julian

Downside Abbey
5 July 1949

Dearest Noreen,

I have just heard that a most <u>charming</u> person (you and she would love each other at once, as she is absolutely natural and unsophisticated, and adores horses!) is arriving in England by air on Friday on a most sad errand.

I knew her when she was Clare Napier-Martin and an officer in the A. T. S. Her mother died at that time, and now her father is dying of cancer and is only expected to live 2 months.

Unfortunately he never forgave her for marrying an American a year ago (though his own wife, whom he loved, was an American), as it meant her going away, and she doesn't know whether even now he will forgive her.

I have always wanted her to meet you as she lives quite near you—Hollow Farm, New Milford, Conn.—and so I was wondering if you would let her come and see you in London now, as I am afraid it is going to be such a sad homecoming for her, and you seem destined to be a comfort to people, as just recently in Lausanne. She will be staying with her cousin, Mrs. Oswald Savage, at 20, Wilton Place. Her married name is Mrs David Burnham, but her husband has broken his ankle and so can't come with her. He is, I believe, a very well known novelist in America, and from her letters sounds one of the kindest and gentlest characters on earth—just like your own husband.

She has promised to come and see me here before she goes back, so I might be able to arrange for you to meet here.

Also, if you are going to the American Embassy, do please look out for my dear friend—James Sappington, from Maryland—I think he is First Secretary; as I have so often told him about you, and he is so longing to meet you.

Fondest love to you both—and you are in my thoughts all day long now that you are so near.

Your affectionate cousin,
Julian

Downside Abbey
26. 7. 49.

Dearest Noreen,

Although this is my busiest week of the year—with 100 priests
from the Plymouth diocese here in retreat and an Old Boys'
cricket-week going on—I am still basking in the joy of your
two-day visit and <u>longing</u> for Thursday; so that three people have
asked me what on earth I am looking so happy about!

I thought it was so sweet of you to write me that lovely letter
before you left Bath. I always think the world has lost so much
by leaving the psalms only to monks and nuns. At Stonor they
used to be sung every day by the six chaplains, so that the family
could take part whenever they were free, and be soothed by those
lovely old shepherd's melodies and the pictures conjured up by
the words of cornfields and vineyards, of flowers and birds, of the
stars at night and the boundless sea.

One thing which is worrying me a bit—I did try to explain
to Johnny, but as he was driving at about sixty miles an hour at
the time, I don't think he really took it in!—is that I must have
given you both the impression (when I was talking about grafting
Christianity on to a communist state) that God <u>meant</u> us all to
be equal and that therefore people like you and Johnny were less
pleasing to God than if you gave away all your possessions and
became poor.

There is, of course, a particular <u>happiness</u> which you miss—the
happiness of someone without anyone depending on him, who
<u>can</u> cease to worry about any earthly possessions and give <u>all</u> his
thoughts to trying to be like Our Lord. And that is why the rich
young man in the gospel was sad—it wasn't Our Lord who was
sad—because he knew he was throwing away the chance of the
supremest <u>happiness</u> that one who loves can have. But it didn't
affect his <u>goodness</u>, which, as Our Lord told him, consisted only
in trying to love God with his whole heart and his neighbor as
himself.

Our Lord never anywhere suggested that riches or other gifts
were <u>wrong</u>, but only that they might be dangerous, if we didn't
see that they were all His <u>gifts</u> to us and so began to think of

them as our own without any thought of Him. But, as long as you realize, as you two both do, that they are 'talents' entrusted to you by God, so far from them being a danger to you, they become a most wonderful means of exercising that love which is the only thing that matters, and at the last judgement you will find that all your talents have multiplied a hundredfold.

It is not chiefly, of course, a matter of money—though, even with that, Johnny could hardly be more generous and kind or give more happiness to everyone around him, from his closest friends to the domestic staff who wait on you. It is much more all your other gifts—your own absolutely breath-taking loveliness, the charm and the happiness that radiate from you both, and all those quite indefinable graces which belong to you both because you are who you are, and which enable you to make people happy by being so natural with them, just as the King and Queen can in England, and which you couldn't do, if you throw those talents away instead of using them, as you <u>are</u> doing.

It is the same all through God's creation. Nowhere has He made everything just the same. There are lots of common, and none the less lovely, flowers, like daisies and buttercups, but He also wanted a few with the breath-taking loveliness of a deep red rose or the grace of a Blue Himalayan poppy. And so it is among the birds, or animals, or wherever you look in his entire creation.

So, though <u>you</u> may not get the supreme happiness of a Saint Francis of Assisi, you more than make up for that by the happiness you are able to <u>give</u>; and, as Our Lord said, it is a more blessed thing to give than to receive.

I <u>must</u> stop now—but I will be seeing you on Thursday. I hope to be at the Ritz about 12—for which hour I am <u>absolutely</u> <u>longing</u>.

My fondest love to you both always—

from Julian

Downside Abbey
28 August 1949

Dearest Noreen,

Your lovely letter—doubly precious from the effort it must have cost you to write it with a house full of guests, who, I can well imagine, want you to be with them from morning till night—reached me on the eve of my birthday. And the book about the mountains arrived a week ago, so that I am now well on it and am loving the descriptions of the climbing. I find it is the simplest things which have left the most vivid and the most precious impressions on my memory—every tiniest detail is still quite distinct in my pictures of rowing our boat at Lulworth while my sisters caught mackerel, and I can visualize every inch of the cliffs as the boat passed them and can almost hear the water gurgling and splashing against them. In the same way I can still picture almost every foot of the way up the various mountains which I climbed with my father and where we saw particular flowers or butterflies and birds.

And, in more recent years, I can, of course, almost feel the warmth of the sun-baked coarse grass on the Warren, with the chalk underneath, and can see, a little further down the slope, the clumps of thistles round the entrances to the rabbit burrows, with brown butterflies fluttering among the thistle-tops, and the distant shade of the beech trees, from which one hopes to see the deer emerging to graze.

It is because it is those simple things, especially when associated inextricably with those we love most, that give us the most precious treasures that remain in our memory for life, that I always hope that God's Providence will yet bring you and Johnny into the peace and loveliness of Turville. It is especially when we are children between the ages of 12 and 18 that the most enduring pictures seem to be stamped on our memories; and, just as I can never think of my father without picturing him as I always saw him in the mountains, so I feel that the most precious thing in the whole world—more precious than any formal 'education'—which you could give Pamela and Nicky, would be the unfading picture of that garden at Turville as the background against which they will always see you and Johnny, and, as they grow older, wonderful rides and picnics in the woods round Stonor with their cousins, and, for Tommy and Nicky, shooting parties with Sherman.

Then, whatever happened to them in after years, they would always have those memories of undiluted happiness. And, of course, the watching of that happiness of theirs—with seven such dream children would make you and Johnny probably the two happiest people on the whole face of the earth.

I know it would mean depriving hundreds of your friends in America of all the happiness they draw from you both now, but the really intimate ones would be able to visit you at Turville and be rewarded by seeing you both in your true setting, and, of course, many, many more friends would soon come flocking to see you from all over England. I am afraid that you will both always suffer from having too many rather than too few friends, for the deepest instinct in human nature is to love what is good and beautiful, and so, since God has showered every imaginable gift and grace on you both, you will never be left alone by people.

Incidentally, talking about your friends, I must tell you that when I left you that evening after that lovely visit to the White City (which I loved most because it completed my picture of you) I went, as I always do on my way to Worth, to see a dear old lady in East Grinstead, whom I have known and loved for years and one of whose daughters I had been able to help when she was having a tragic time during the war. I told her I had just come from the White City; whereupon she said how she wished I had met her other daughter there and her granddaughter, Jane—and so I discovered that the other daughter, whom I had only heard talked about by her Christian name hitherto, was your Mrs Kent. In the end I had to spend the night there, as I missed the last bus out to Worth.

Another coincidence when I left you was to find that your driver, who was so full of admiration for you both, was a Catholic whose only sister I had known well when she was a maid here before the war and who is now in hospital with T. B.—but will be cured by the spring.

It is extraordinary how those sort of coincidences always seem to pursue me, because when I got to Victoria and into a dingy little carriage on the local train to East Grinstead, who should get in but my greatest friend when I was at school—Edmund Howard—who was over for a brief holiday from the British Embassy in Rome.

My family always maintain that they have never yet seen me get into a train or bus without someone immediately saying: "Fancy meeting you here!"

I am afraid I wasn't able to get to Stonor, as they couldn't spare me from Worth; but Worth was a real holiday—including two local gymkhanas, at one of which an old friend of mine, Sam Marsh, turned out to be another of your most devoted admirers! On the strength of that he insisted on my arranging for him to give a free course of lectures and demonstrations to the boys at Worth. But I am hoping to go to Stonor later in the year, as I must arrange about the illustrations for the book with Sherman. The printing has gone right ahead, as soon as I told them of Johnny's sweet offer, but I am afraid it won't be ready by Christmas.

If you don't go earlier, do try and go to the Sunday Vespers at Portsmouth on one of the Sundays in Advent (November 27th to Christmas), as the Office then is particularly lovely. And, of course, give my love to Father Gregory, who I know will be very thrilled to meet you.

I feel I must apologize for the length of this letter, but I felt that as it was my birthday I would hide myself away from all guests for an hour or two and just talk to you. With my fondest love to you both and to darling Pamela and Nicky, and of course my heart is still brimming over with gratitude to you and Johnny for all the lovely memories you both gave me during this last visit.

always your affectionate
Julian

Downside Abbey
August 28th 1949

MY DEAREST PAMELA,

YOUR LOVELY LETTER, WHICH ARIVED JUST IN TIME FOR MY BIRTHDAY, WAS A MOST WONDERFUL SURPRISE.

THE GOAT IS QUITE GROWN-UP NOW AND HAS A LITTLE BABY OF ITS OWN. AND, WHAT YOU WOULD LOVE JUST AS MUCH AS THE BABY GOAT, THE BEAGLES (THE DOGS YOU SAW) HAVE GOT TWO FAMILIES OF PUPPIES (FOURTEEN ALTOGETHER), WHICH ARE A MONTH OLD AND JUST LEARNING TO WALK AND PLAY. YOU WILL BE ABLE TO GUESS WHAT THEY ARE LIKE FROM THE DARLING ONE THAT MUMMY BROUGHT BACK WITH HER.

I SO LOVED SEEING HER AND DADDY WHEN THEY CAME OVER THIS SUMMER. THEY ARE THE TWO PEOPLE I LOVE MOST IN THE WORLD. BUT I WISH YOU HAD COME AGAIN TOO. YOU WOULD HAVE LOVED SOME LITLE PONIES WHICH MUMMY TOOK ME TO SEE IN LONDON, SOME OF THEM BEING RIDDEN BY LITTLE GIRLS YOUNGER THAN YOU.

I DO HOPE YOU COME WITH THEM NEXT YEAR, AND NICKY AS WELL. I HAD TO COME BACK FROM MY LOVELY ISLAND, AND I DON'T THINK I WILL EVER BE ABLE TO GO AND LIVE THERE NOW. BUT, TO MAKE UP, I WILL BE ABLE TO SEE MUCH MORE OF YOU, WHENEVER YOU COME TO ENGLAND.

WITH VERY MUCH LOVE TO YOU BOTH, AND THANK YOU VERY MUCH FOR YOUR LOVELY BIRTHDAY LETTER.
GOD BLESS YOU ALWAYS—
COUSIN JULIAN

Downside Abbey
18 Dec. 1949.

Dearest Noreen and Johnny,

I hope this will be in time to bring to you both my fondest love and blessing for Christmas night.

I never have time to write private letters nowadays, because, on top of the Abbot's ones (which run into hundreds a day at this time of year) and the guests, I now have yet another job—and one which I love so much that I find every hour which I have to spend away from it almost unbearable.

Because I have been put in charge of a large scattered parish—partly coal-miners and partly farming villagers—about nine miles from here. It has been terribly neglected for 25 years, so that when I took it over on October 1st there were only fifty Catholics, half of whom never came to church and were only names on a list. But by going out there, every evening I can, from about 7 to 11, I have already gathered a flock of 160, including 75 children, most of them really lovely families.

I have now made a second church at the other end of the parish in the little village of Wellow, called after St Julian's Well. And by great luck we found the two halves of the old Catholic font—about 1,000 years old—and put it together (it had lain half-buried for 400 years since it was broken at the Reformation)—and the very first baby which was presented to be baptized was called Julian, though the parents knew nothing about St Julian's Well (from which we drew the water) or about the old parish church from which the font came having been dedicated to St Julian.

That particular St Julian was a hermit at Wellow in Roman days and belonged to the same dark Celtic race as our ancestors at Stonor, so I am sure he is helping me from heaven, because most wonderful things seem to happen every day, some of them almost miraculous. I am longing for you to see the little church next summer, and it is a most lovely unspoilt village.

I do hope you will have some minutes of peace away from all your guests and friends at Christmas—in which to think of the little new-born Lamb of God, born in the midst of all the

thousands of little new-born lambs, which were always kept at
Bethlehem for the Temple sacrifices, and please whisper a prayer
to Him for me—

always your affectionate Julian

"I myself will visit my sheep, saith the Lord God".

With all my love to you both for Christmas 1949,
Julian

Downside Abbey
8 March 1950

Dearest Noreen,

At last I have managed to get a free hour, owing to my car being in dock, in which to try and thank you for your really lovely letter of nearly a month ago and to tell you anything I can about Aunt Julie's death.

(Incidentally, I have just had a telegram from Jeanne to tell me that her mother died yesterday).

I gather that Aunt Julie's death couldn't have been more peaceful, and her mind remained as clear as ever to the end, although she was nearly ninety.

I only managed to get there in time for the actual burial in the little Pishill cemetery—between her mother and Harry. A big crowd of people had been to the Requiem Mass in the chapel, but only a handful came to the actual burial—mostly relations—and it was a lovely still morning of early spring.

Afterwards I had one of the happiest days at Stonor I have ever had, because Sherman and Jeanne seemed so much happier together, and Sherman was at his very nicest, when, as you know, only Johnny can compare with him for kindness and generosity. How I was wishing you could have been with us when he took me out to show me all his new Guernsey cows and the new stalls he is making for them in what used to be your main stable. Now that the scars are healed where he had removed the evergreens and the hedge in front of the house, it is all looking lovelier than ever before, and, as for the children, no words could describe how lovely they are.

Owing to your dear Johnny's generosity, I hope the book really will be out this summer. The proofs have been corrected and all the illustrations are ready, except for a drawing by John Piper of the tomb at Dorchester, which he has promised for this week. I found rather a nice coloured photograph by Cecil Roberts for the frontispiece.

How I wish I could find time to put down in writing for you the book about the Old and New Testaments which I have always longed to write. If I ever do, it will be dedicated to you.

The nuns at Talacre, to whom I preached it for a retreat in the autumn, have implored me to let them type it out so as to get it published, so, if I get ill again, I really will think about it. They say it is just exactly what so many people, like your Macauley friends, are longing for.

But, at present there is no possibility of my even beginning to get it into writing as, on top of the guests and the Abbot's letters, I now have this large parish of which I told you. I love it more and more, especially the <u>eighty</u> children, mostly under the age of seven, whom I am longing to show you when you next come.

It has naturally been a <u>very</u> great disappointment learning that you will probably not be coming over this summer, but I can quite understand how you will be longing to go back to Merrymount after six months in New York. But oh! How I wish it could have been Turville instead of Merrymount, if only the times we live in hadn't been so desperately difficult and expensive.

But I know God will bless you both more than ever for sacrificing such day-dreams for the sake of those two precious children He has entrusted to you, just as you have sacrificed Merrymount as a home for the sake of their education. And I am sure that Aunt Julie, who so loved that paradise of beauty which she had been able to make out of a few fields on this temporary earth, will see to it that there is an infinitely more lovely home awaiting you one day in the real world which is going to last for ever and ever and ever, and where distances will mean no more than they do here to our thoughts, which can flash across the Atlantic in a split second.

How strange to think that she is now young again, never to grow old, and radiantly lovely. All that was loveliest in her character could only dimly make itself felt while she was on earth. We caught glimpses of it in the beauty she created and loved at Turville, but most of it was hidden even from herself by the veils of inherited character, surroundings in her youth dominated by others, childlessness, loneliness and advancing age, etc. etc.

So it must be with all of us while we are leading our caterpillar-life on earth, and no one feels the weight of those earthly surroundings more than you yourself. But when God gives us our particular cross to bear He sees already the 'Butterfly' in all its dazzling beauty which is already latent in the crawling earth-bound caterpillar and which will one day emerge into the world of eternal sunshine for which it was created, flying where it will from flower to flower and living only on honey. <u>He</u> knows the feelings of frustration and uselessness which you sometimes feel, and He knows that it is really a homesickness for Him and for the true happiness which He has in store for you and for which He has created you. For He made you for Himself, and your heart will always be restless until it finally rests in the vision of His beauty and the realization of His love.

With my fondest love to you both and to the children—

Julian

Downside Abbey
18 Oct 1950

Dearest Noreen,

Ever since your lovely birthday letter I have been longing to
write to you, but wanted to have time to write a real letter and
not just a scribble. But I see now that I will have to wait now
for another illness before that happens, and so your postcard of
yesterday has filled me with remorse.

The difficulty is that I am out in my parish from early morning until about ten every night and when I do get back I always
have at least two hours of prayers to make up, that I have missed
during the day and which have to be said before midnight, and
then, what with business letters and correcting the final proofs
of the book, I am always so tired that I have to lie down for a
few hours before starting my next day at five.

Actually I have never felt so well, as I simply love the work in
the parish, for it is so true what Our Lord said that it is a more
blessed thing to give than to receive, and on a parish it is 'give
give give' all the time. The children are still my greatest joy, and I
now have 150 of them for the 30 I found this time last year. I am
longing for you to see them when you come next summer—and,
oh, how I am longing to see you—and the whole family this time.
Do thank your darling Pam for her perfectly charming birthday
letter which I will treasure almost as much as yours.

I was hoping that the book would have been out in time for
Christmas but, alas, a printer's strike has delayed it a little longer.
It has 400 pages and lots of illustrations, including most of the
ones that have been appearing in Country Life.

Has Sherman sent you a copy of the Country Life articles? If
not, I would love to, as I have been given several copies.

I am so looking forward to meeting the Macauleys, as it will
make you seem so much closer to be with friends of yours. I know
a lovely Tudor farmhouse near London where they keep about a
dozen nice horses and run a sort of guest house, especially for
families with children, so I think it would suit them for weekends. And I do hope they will come here very often. I am sure
Mr. Sappington will love to drive them down.

I spent two insides of a week at Stonor in the summer—when the children were suspected of polio—the children themselves were even lovelier than ever, and I had a wonderful day with Julia and Thomas at the Henley Horse Show, but, oh! how we <u>longed</u> for you to be there. Mrs Kent & Jane were there, but not Mr. Tatlow. And my greatest joy of all was that Jeanne put me in <u>your</u> room each time.

On the 23rd of this month one of my parishioners is taking me to Rome by air for the Holy Year. It will only be a week—Saturday to Saturday—but will be a most wonderful experience, because we will be in Rome when the Pope proclaims the doctrine of the Assumption, which will be an amazing spectacle, and the very next day we fly to London for two days on the way back. I will, of course, remember you and Johnny very often in both places.

With my fondest love to you both and to the children, and please forgive me for the pain I caused you—

God bless you always—

Julian

LETTERS
1951–55

Downside Abbey
11 April 1951

Dearest Noreen,

I have, of course, been thinking of you almost hourly as you drew nearer and I imagine that by today you are near enough for me to write to you.

I don't think I will be able to get away to see you at Stonor, which is, of course, what I would love most, because, except on Saturdays, I am tied every day at 9 a.m. and 4 p.m., as I have to fetch my eight most scattered children to and from school in my car, as the coaches can't reach their villages.

But if you could come down to Bath again, any week would be the same for me—whichever fits in best with your plans.

I am so longing for you to see some of the children—and for them to see you!—and the little church which we built at Wellow last summer. And also to tell you of my extraordinary adventures in Rome and Lourdes in November. But, most of all, I am just longing to see you both again—it seems more like ten years since you were here.

With my very fondest love to you both and praying that you will enjoy every hour of your visit and get back just a little of the joy you will both give—

always your affectionate
Julian

The Presbytery
Egremont
Cumberland
27 Sept. 1951

My dearest Noreen,

So much has happened since the day you sailed away on the Queen Elizabeth that I have been waiting and waiting for a really free hour in which I could sit down and write to you, and only now has it come. I won't tell the reason why I have got an hour now, or you won't read the rest of the letter!

The very day you sailed I had a very sad blow, as I was told that I had to leave my beloved Peasedown and Wellow and come up here to help the priest here who is getting old and has a weak chest. I was given a month's notice, and I think it was the most agonizing month I have ever passed in my life. Not only was there the pain of all the goodbyes, but there was a dreadful anxiety about the future as the Abbot wouldn't believe my numbers and I heard that he wasn't going to send a priest to take my place but get two aged nuns to come out from Bath once a month in a bus, who, of course, wouldn't have been able to visit more than a handful of the people.

However, behind my back the parishioners started making petitions to him and to the Bishop and at the very end the Abbot realized that he was wrong and what a tragedy it would be to let those 150 small children lose the faith in Our Lord which they had just received, and when I went to say goodbye to him he not only apologized for having made everything so difficult for me, but quite overwhelmed me by telling me that he was appointing three priests to take my place, one of them to be free of all other duties whatsoever.

And now I have found myself up here, more than three hundred miles from Downside or Stonor—in fact there is a lovely view of Scotland from the parish. It is the wildest and loveliest country in England—all mountains and lakes and wonderful people, but there is a desperate amount to be done, as the priest has been an invalid for years and hasn't done any visiting for many months. And unfortunately the shingles have come back to my right eye—for ten days I have been hoping it wasn't a real attack and have been working desperately hard to get the most urgent things done in case it should get worse, but this morning the eye has closed up altogether and I am looking as sinister a sight as when poor Johnny saw me with it at Worth, so I am waiting till the doctor's surgery opens at 11, and so have found this hour in which to write my belated thanks to you for the unforgettable day you gave me last summer and for your sweet birthday letter.

And I must again thank Johnny for his wonderful generosity over the book. The first edition is expected to be sold out in another week or two, which will have paid for the costs of production, and so I don't think there will be any need for us to take advantage of his lovely generous offer. The publisher is now preparing a second edition, all the profits from which he is allowing to go to the upkeep of the Chapel.

If, like last time, I am sent away to convalesce after the shingles, I will write another book—for you only—the one I have always promised you on the Old and New Testaments. And it will be even more a labour of love than the one on Stonor.

About your question as to keeping holy the Sabbath day—there are two quite distinct commandments, one of which has long ago been absorbed into the other.

In the old Jewish law they had to keep the Sabbath ('seventh')[1] day holy by resting from all servile work. If we still kept the Jewish law, we would therefore have to rest from all servile work on Saturdays. But now that the Redemption has been accomplished, the Church has made her own holy day, which quite naturally is the day of the Resurrection—Sunday—which she means to be a day of rejoicing, a holiday, and one on which we are absolutely free to go to Mass and afterwards spend the day in rejoicing. I never quite know what the position is for Christians outside the Catholic Church. They are obviously not bound by the old Jewish penitential law, but nor do they seem to be bound by the law which the Catholic Church has made for her subjects. I would say that all you ought to do is to allow your maids the opportunity to go to church sometime on the Sunday, if they want to, and, as far as circumstances allow, try to make Sunday an easier day for them.

---

1   The etymology of the word "Sabbath" for the seventh day of the Jewish week is from the day for "rest," not for the number "seven."

I am sorry this has been a rather formal sounding letter, but I am writing it with one eye on the clock, which is very near 11.

I don't think myself the shingles are going to prove nearly so bad this time, being the second time on the same nerve—I certainly <u>feel</u> much better than last time—but if I do have to go to hospital for a bit, I promise you I will send you cards from time to time, so <u>please</u> don't worry and start telephoning or calling or anything like that.

Do please give my fondest love to dear Johnny, and to your darling Pamela and Nicky, whose photographs are the joy of my life; and you know that you yourself hold an absolutely unique place in my heart and I can never thank God enough for having let me know you (I have never even <u>seen</u> your sister!)

always your affectionate
Julian

[Postcard]   Cumberland
                                    12 Oct 1951

   Am well on the road to recovery and back at work. The lake
pictured on the other side is right in the centre of my parish.
There is a nice hotel (part 13th century, part 16th) a few miles
from it, with 12 horses & ponies, sea-bathing two miles away and
salmon fishing at the door; so I am already wondering whether I
will be able to tempt you to bring up the children for a few days
next summer. Fondest love to you all, Julian

The Presbytery
Egremont
Cumberland
17 Dec 1951

Dearest Noreen,

I have an awful feeling that I should be sending this to Fifth
Avenue, but can't quite make out from your last letter whether
you have actually closed Merrymount yet. I do hope you are <u>not</u>
in New York, as there are terrible descriptions of the cold there
in our papers. At any rate, wherever you are, I, of course, wish you
all a very, very happy Christmas together. And how I am <u>longing</u>
to see you all in the New Year! If your darling Pamela goes on
looking lovelier and lovelier in all her photographs she really will
be challenging your place in my heart one day. It will be so lovely
to see Julia and Pamela together, now that they are growing so
alike; to my mind they are both so perfect and their characters
so match their lovely open faces that one glance at a snapshot
of either of them is enough to dispel any moods of depression
that I get into. My favourite one of Pamela, and of Nicky too,
is the one where Nicky is flat out on the sand with Pamela and
another girl sitting on him; the whole essence of the happiness
of childhood is reflected in their faces, and one realizes what a
world without any evil is going to be like in heaven.

But, oh, how I always wish people had taken more snapshots
of <u>you</u> when you were that age and were just as carefree on the
back of a pony in the park.

I am getting to love the people up here—though they are not, of
course, <u>mine</u>, as were the people at Peasedown and Wellow, especially all the children. Here I am only a curate in someone else's
parish, and I am afraid I still feel terribly frustrated and thwarted
at every turn. There is so much I would love to do, but can't. However, the country is breathtakingly lovely in the distant parts of
the parish and that, together with the photographs of Pamela and
Nicky, does a great deal to console me and help me to be patient.

At present I am being inundated with very sorrowful letters
from Peasedown and Wellow, as Downside gave up all responsibility
for them a few weeks ago and although the Bishop has appointed

his best priest from Bath to step into the breach, he can't do so much as the monks could and there seems to be a real danger of Wellow being closed down after Christmas.

I find it so hard to understand how really <u>good</u> and holy people can be so blind to the needs of others. There was such a hunger for God in those two villages and, as you know, they were so thrilled by it all. It is especially those 150 children, whom I had the joy of baptizing and preparing for their First Communion, that now fill me with anxiety.

And here it is much the same; the parish priest hasn't done any visiting for 8 or 9 years and I have found more than a hundred forgotten Catholics in the remoter farms and valleys; but I am not allowed to do anything for them and find it very hard to visit them even once a month as he won't allow me to use the car, which only leaves the garage twice a week when he goes to lunch with neighbouring priests—and so it has taken me exactly three months to cover 750 miles on the bicycle, which I would have done in a week in my last parish. In Egremont itself I, of course, prefer being on foot, as somehow one can't imagine Our Lord or His apostles in cars even if they had lived in the 20th century, but these hill people and their children on the distant farms have been so neglected and it is not their fault that they have to live miles and miles from a church.

I am so sorry for this outburst, especially in a Christmas letter.

My last letter from Sherman was much more happy and optimistic than usual. I am hoping that soon the book will be making its contribution towards doing up the Chapel, because the second edition is selling quite well and it continues to get nothing but very kind and friendly reviews. Do please thank Johnny once more for his generous offer which alone made it possible.

With my fondest love and blessings to you all—

from Julian

The Presbytery
Egremont
Cumberland
1 Jan 1952

My darling Noreen—

I had already loved your first letter, but the second one has moved me so much that I just don't know what to say. Ever since I first met you I have, of course, known that even if you had been my twin sister I couldn't have loved you more, and yet that love grows deeper and deeper with the years.

Your second letter coming so quickly on the heels of the first has, I am sure, enabled me to know exactly what our great ancestor, Saint Thomas More, felt in what was surely the most moving moment of his life. No one else had ever held quite the same place in his affections as his eldest daughter Margaret. I did put one incident about her in the 'Stonor' book, but I wish now that I had put this other, as so much of the book was really written for you, and she was your great-great-great aunt.

On his way back to the Tower after being condemned to death she was allowed to say goodbye to him. She wrote in her diary that she managed by a superhuman effort to do so without breaking down, but that, a few moments later, when he was being led on again, she could no longer bear it, and, rushing through the guards, threw her arms round his neck, sobbing out: "My father! O my father!" She could see the agony it caused him, but afterwards for the rest of her life she treasured the last little note he was able to write her the next day, scribbled with a piece of charcoal. For in it he wrote that he had never loved her more than when at that last meeting her daughterly love had paid no heed to all the bystanders but had spoken straight to his heart.

Incidentally, in the second edition of the book, which should be out any day now, there are several new discoveries, including the arrest and imprisonment for ten long years of the wife, the sister and the daughter of that unheroic Sir Francis Stonor, whose mother had died in prison and whose younger brother was exiled for life. It is most striking how much more heroic and loyal the women were than the men, just as they were at the time of Our Lord's crucifixion.

54

With my fondest love and blessing, and thank you a thousand times for writing that loveliest of letters. May this new year bring you all four happiness and blessings beyond anything you could desire. Already I am being thrilled by the thought that before it is half over I will be seeing you all—

always your affectionate
Julian

The Presbytery
Egremont
Cumberland
30 May 1952

Dearest Noreen,

Thank you very much for your kind thought in sending me the telegram. I had been so hoping that you were safely installed at Bockmer and had, of course, meant to have a letter there waiting to welcome you.

I do hope that you will both <u>really</u> <u>relax</u> there now, especially when Pamela and Nicky come on the 10th, and be really firm and strong about refusing all the invitations and engagements, which take up so much of your time in America. You must have seen so many beautiful things in Portugal, Rome and Greece (I don't ever feel very attracted by Turkey), and met so many people, that any more sight-seeing in England would only be an anti-climax, so do, please, drop right back into the slow-moving world to which Bockmer and Stonor really belong—I am sure that what would really do you most good would be to cut the telephone wires, lock your car away in a garage and limit yourself to the speed and distance that you can ride on a horse!

I had been hoping very much to be with you in June. Jeanne has pressed me so warmly to come to her birthday party, though I am quite out of my depths on such occasions, and June must be such a lovely month in the Chilterns; but the parish priest is not fit to carry on alone and it has proved impossible to get another priest from Downside to take my place until after the Abbot's visit here in the last week in June. There <u>will</u> be one coming on July 9th for a fortnight, so I am hoping to be able to leave here on Monday, July 7th and to stay till Friday the 25th, dividing the time between Stonor and Bockmer. I am sure it will be the happiest fortnight in the whole of my life. I have always so longed to see you as you were as a child, riding through the woods in your oldest pair of jodhpurs and brightening the lives of all the old keepers and woodmen whom you met or stopping to talk to their wives in their cottages, who all obviously loved you with a quite special love which none of the rest of the family inspired.

I am hoping to find you doing just the same this summer, and there will be the added joy of seeing all the seven children together, with Julia and Pamela looking just as I have always imagined you, and Nicky to be seen for the first time in my life, though I already feel I have known him always, so often have I looked at your snapshots of him which you gave me, and prayed for more and more blessings on his head.

With my fondest love to you both—

Julian

The Presbytery
Egremont
Cumberland
6 July 1952

My dearest Noreen,

Each day I have put off writing to you, hoping to have some more definite plans, but in the end I can see I will have to telegraph or telephone.

One of the things the Abbot insisted on at his visitation last week was that I should be given a car, since the parish priest is in bed on more days than not and doesn't like me using his; and if he is willing and able to get me one before Wednesday, then of course I may be able to come down in it.

Otherwise, the earliest I can reach London (Euston) by train is 7.30 in the evening, so I am afraid I may be rather late by the time I reach Marlow. I have no means of looking up a train here, but I will go straight across to Paddington and take the next one.

I do hope that, now that Henley is over, you will be able to relax completely during this coming week. Certainly, once I am under your roof, nothing will induce me to go further afield than Stonor.

I still can't believe that in a few hours I will actually be staying with you in your own house and seeing you all together as a family. And of course I am longing for my first sight of Nicky, and to see that darling Pamela again, who last time was an adorable little girl without any front teeth.

I will send you a telegram the moment I know definitely how I am coming—with all my love—and I am feeling just as excited as any small child!

from
Julian

The Presbytery

Egremont

Cumberland

Sunday, July 27th

Dearest Noreen,

I still can't believe that there are hundreds of miles separating us once more, and I would be feeling dreadfully sad if it were not for the thought of seeing you here so soon and showing you this lovely country. As it was, I nearly disgraced myself at one period towards the end of the Horse Show when I realized that it was the last day I would be seeing Pamela and Nicky, and I had to retire among the horse boxes until I could get rid of the lump in my throat and an acute danger of tears.

The Sella Park Hotel will, I know, welcome you at any time, though among the seven hospital cases that I found awaiting me here were Mrs Rose (the owner's wife and, at present, the cook) and Mrs McVarish, the wife of their Highland gardener, so that they are a bit disorganized there.

Would a slightly later date in August be at all possible for you both? Because my parish priest is going away for a holiday tomorrow (he proposes, among other things, to visit Stonor!), and has arranged for me to have what is known as the Forty Hours' Adoration from Sunday to Tuesday, August 10th to 12th, which means that I will have to be in the church practically non-stop on August 9th, 10th, 11th & 12th, and would hardly see you at all and wouldn't be able to show you any of the lakes and mountains.

It is looking so <u>heavenly</u> now, so fresh and green and the air so soft and scented that in some ways I am tempted to suggest your coming before the 9th, but it wouldn't give Anne Clifford time to give me her Scottish suggestions—unless you went on to Scotland for those four hectic days (9th–12th).

When you do come up, do <u>insist</u> on the A. A. people planning your route for the last part of the journey to Egremont through the inland northern route—Carnforth, Kendal, Keswick, Cockermouth (<u>don't</u> take the Egremont road in the middle of Cockermouth High Street, but the Whitehaven one), Whitehaven, North Circular Road, Egremont.

With my fondest love to you all and, of course, more gratitude than I can ever possibly put into words for the love you both—or rather you all four—showered on me.

I do hope <u>your</u> eye is better, because mine is! Bless you all at every moment!

Julian

The Presbytery
Egremont
31 July 1952

Dearest Noreen,

There has been such a rush since I came back that I have hardly had time to breathe, but the thought of your coming visit keeps me going when things seem extra impossible.

Anne says that Inverailort would be impossible during those middle weeks of August as it will be crowded out with guests for the grouse shooting.

She suggests that if you are only spending two nights in Scotland that it would be best to spend the Saturday night at Oban on the west coast, opposite the island of Mull, and the Sunday night in Edinburgh, from which you would have the best run south, straight down the Great North Road, which avoids all the big cities. There are very good hotels in both places, but August is the most popular month in Scotland, when all the heather is out, and so it would be as well to ring up as soon as possible any hotels marked with 3 or 4 stars in the A. A. guide book.

In great haste to catch the post but my thoughts will be with you all the time the letter is on the way,

your affectionate
Julian

Egremont
Monday, Sept 1st

My dearest Noreen,

I have spent a most awful weekend trying in vain to find a way round a dreadful obstacle which has suddenly presented itself.

I learnt on Saturday that one of the priests at Cleator, who are always willing to say a mass for us here if we are a priest short, is suddenly being moved this Wednesday to be a parish priest in Northumberland and his successor is not expected for about a fortnight. I have tried everywhere I can think of to get another priest, but to no avail, and so I have had to cancel the retreat at Worth and my last glimpse of all of you. You can imagine how forlorn I am feeling.

I feel sure I will be seeing you and Johnnie again in a few months—and I hope it will be in the heavenly setting of Caldey—but I suppose it will be years before I see the two adorable children again.

I will go on trying, and even if I can get away for one day I will, of course, send you a telegram at once.

With all my love—
Julian

The Presbytery
Egremont
22 October 1952

My dearest Noreen,

It is so nice to know your birthday at last, and I do wish you a very very happy one on Sunday. Even now I may have left this letter too late as I don't know whether you will be spending it in New York or with your mother at Portsmouth. At any rate, wherever you are, you know I will be spending most of the day, whatever I am doing, begging God in my heart to bless you and bring you nearer and nearer to Himself.

I had a very nice letter from Nurse Bradley the other day, and I had a short weekend at Stonor fairly recently to talk over Charles's future with Archbishop Mathew, who was staying there; otherwise last summer has already begun to seem very remote. But, luckily, that isn't true of your visit up here, and every time I come to a place which I saw with you and Johnny, it only seems last week that you were here.

I couldn't think what to send you as a token of remembrance for your birthday until I saw a sweet picture of the Queen with 'David' and 'Pearl' on the cover of Picture Post, so have asked the publishers to send it to you.

With my fondest love and blessings to you all four,
your affectionate
Julian

Egremont

31 May 1953

Dearest Noreen,

I am so touched by your wonderful generosity in facing those two long night journeys and all the expenses involved, in order to give me the wonderful joy of seeing you all three again. But how I <u>wish</u> Sella Park wasn't being sold this week, as, although the Drummonds professed to be quite satisfied with their month at the Scawfell Hotel, I am afraid it isn't a patch on the other and I am very much afraid that your two days there may be rather an ordeal for you.

The only thing that decided me is its handiness for you at your arrival. You just walk out of the little station at Seascale and there it is opposite you and you will be able to have a hot breakfast right away. And it has the reputation of being the next best after Sella Park.

The car, an Austin 8, comes from a garage just a few yards up the village, but I am afraid it is rather expensive, as he charges £5 for three days, exclusive of petrol. It really is so good of Johnny to do all this. Incidentally the owner said would he please make sure to bring his driving-license.

Perhaps if you find the hotel too uncomfortable—your rooms didn't look very comfortable to me, though Pam is next to you down a little passage on the side away from the railway and looking towards the hills—and I haven't been able, in two attempts, to catch the manager in to ask for the bathroom in that passage to be reserved for you—the secretary would only say that that was never done, but that in practice no one else would be likely to use it—so if you find it too uncomfortable, it might be better for you to move on the Saturday or Sunday to a bigger hotel—say the Crown & Mitre at Carlisle, as you will be going from there on the Sunday evening.

The first day, Friday, will be the only day I will really be able to see very much of you. I won't be able to be there when you actually arrive, as on Fridays I take communion to all the sick after my Mass, but I hope to be with you by 10 in the morning and to be able to keep the whole of the rest of that day free.

On Saturday I have confessions all the morning until 12, but will be free in the middle part of the day from 12 till 6, after which I have confessions for the rest of the evening.

On Sunday I am in church without a break from 8 till 12, and that evening we have our Corpus Christi procession from 6 till 8, so that I won't actually be able to see you off.

But I am absolutely <u>longing</u> to see you and am feeling overwhelmed with gratitude at the generosity of you both in coming so far for such a short time.

with my <u>fondest</u> love—
your affectionate
Julian

The Presbytery
Egremont
Cumberland
13 July 1953

My dearest Noreen,

I don't think a day has passed since you left that I haven't made a resolution that, whatever happened, I would write to you and Johnnie, and yet it has taken me five weeks! If only it wasn't so much harder to write than it is to talk, you would have had a long letter every day, there is so much that I keep wishing you were here for me to tell you.

But today everything has come together to make me write—in the first place your own letter (yours are the only ones which I still read over and over again, however busy I am); then the disquieting news in it about your father (do please give him my very special love and a promise to remember him in my Mass every day); then it was at this time last year that I was with you at Bockmer and so I have been keeping the photographs in front of me to help me to re-live it all; and, finally, today is the feast of the Benedictine nun, Saint Mildred, who is really your patron saint and who I think must have come from Cumberland as it seems to be the only county where her feast is still kept.

Every time I see you both I realize that I love you more; but this time I felt completely overcome by your wonderful generosity in giving me so much of your very short visit to England, and spending two whole nights in the train so as to make the visit three times longer. Where Johnnie is concerned all ordinary standards of generosity simply lose their meaning, but I simply don't dare try to work out what those three days and nights must have cost him. I am sure there must be very very few people in the world who leave such a train of real happiness behind them wherever they go.

It was our Lord Himself who said that it is a more blessed thing to give than to receive, but oh! how rare it is to find someone who has really penetrated to the secret of that blessedness. Either there is a slight grudgingness or a slight condescension or, in the case of professionally 'religious' people, a slight smugness;

66

but Johnnie always does it <u>so</u> perfectly and for the most natural reasons in the world—because the little serving maid at the Bourn House really was so pretty and unspoiled and so anxious to please or the Austrian one at the Burn Moor feeling rather homesick and so on hour after hour and day after day. He saves them from every trace of humiliation because he really does make them feel that they must have done their part well and earned something and that the size of the present is just because he is such a kind and generous person.

It was only when I got into the house that I discovered that his present to me was exactly twice the amount I had thought and which had already made me break down, and so my last defences crumbled and, though I didn't actually <u>shed</u> tears, my eyes were full of them.

I have felt I owed it to him to use it only in cases where there was no other means of help open, but they didn't take long to come. Ten days ago four of my Catholic miners were crushed to death by a roof fall in the Beckermet iron-ore mine and one of them was an Italian who hadn't quite completed his two-year contract and so, by some wretched regulations, his young wife, Teresa, gets no compensation from the State! Poor girl she was definitely devoted to him, as she is an orphan and had never really known what happiness was until she married him last Christmas. She had come over here to work in an Italian café at Whitehaven where she met him, and he was the most charming man—quiet and always smiling and cheerful. She is having her first baby at the end of this month, which, now, alas, he will never see, but I hope it will distract her from her grief, as she still does nothing but sit indoors crying. She can't speak a word of English, but I am able to talk to her through another very nice young Italian wife whom I take in with me and, as Johnnie's steward, have been able to promise her that she can get all the clothes she needs for the baby, and a very good and kind Catholic maternity sister is looking after her.

The second case was an old nurse out in Eskdale. For 44 years she had been the devoted 'companion' to a dear but very impoverished old lady who died this week. Owing to a spendthrift brother, now dead, the old lady was 'kept' by the estate through a solicitor and had understood that if she died first the estate would also 'keep' her nurse, who had been with her so long and is now 81. But the day the old lady died, the solicitor stopped the payment and wrote to tell the nurse that she must find her own help from that day forward and must be out of the house in three weeks. Luckily I have been able to get her into a lovely home in Harrogate, but again it was wonderful to be able through Johnnie, to see her through these three weeks, as she has spent every penny of her own money buying things for the old lady during her long illness, as she always understood that the estate would help her when the time came.

The five-day riding tour seems about as long ago as your visit, but that too was absolutely perfect. I have written a proper account, with lots of photographs, which I will send to you when I get them back from my cousin, who is using them to write an article for "Country Life". Every minute of it was perfect and far more lovely than we had ever dreamed.

I haven't forgotten the medal of St. Nicholas; and I have discovered two of the Gregorian chant records—they are His Master's Voice D. 1971 & 1972; they are not the two I heard at Downside, but I think you will love them. I have also got a few papers for Nadine, but there are so many books and papers on the Coronation now that it is difficult to choose and I imagine she won't want too many. The two best seem to be "Country Life" and the "Tatler", with one lovely coloured picture in "Illustrated".

Please thank Nicky very much for his letter, and with my fondest love and blessing to you all four—from

Julian

Egremont
Cumberland
10 Sept. 1953

My dearest Noreen,

I am so glad about the muddle which brought me two birthday letters from you, as well as a perfectly sweet one from Pam. And even the family news was all good for once, that your father is a little better in spite of the great heatwave that has made news even in our papers, that Sherman is buying Bosmore off you, and that Wingrove is returning to you.

The Bragas haven't called in here yet, so I expect they went up to Scotland by the Great North Road which doesn't come within a hundred miles of Egremont.

It was such a joy to learn that you too had fallen under the spell of Cumberland. I have come to love it so much that I am now hoping that I will never be moved and the only holiday I have bothered to take this year was the three days with you and the 5-day riding tour immediately afterwards, and, if it wasn't for all my relations being in the south, I would be only too glad to spend all my holidays in the Fells.

October 25th

For weeks I have been hoping to add to this letter in order to get it off in time for your birthday, and I have also been longing to write one to darling Pam, who has been so sweet about writing and sending me things. But I haven't had a chance to write any private letters for two months.

October 26th

Here is the day itself and I still haven't got any further, because the visitor who interrupted me stayed till 11.30, which only left me half an hour to finish off my Offices for the day (always rather long on Sundays) before midnight, and then to say the first two hours of today's Office (said, of course, for you), which I always make a rule that it will be the first task of each day. So it is two in the morning when I am starting this, and at least the first three hours of your birthday will have been devoted uninterruptedly to you.

I don't think even I have ever been quite so desperately busy

November 1st

No sooner had I written the words than there was a knock on my window and one of his neighbors brought me a message that one of my best parishioners who has had two successive strokes seemed to be sinking fast. (Actually he has rallied since then and seems to be holding his own, but I had to sit with him that morning until Mass-time, because he might have died at any moment).

Since then I haven't had another moment to think of letter-writing, but though it made me feel dreadful all day on your birthday to think of you getting no letter from me, at least most of my occupations that day were ones that left you vividly before my mind. Because after Mass I went up to Carlisle by train and walked to the hospital where I said goodbye to you the time before last and where I had two people to see, and then back to the station where I was to meet Archbishop Mathew on his way south from Scotland. As we had planned, we talked for half an hour or so in the station and then I travelled with him for the Cumberland part of his journey.

Almost all our conversation was of Stonor, where he had been staying again only three weeks before, and he is very devoted to Sherman and longs, like all of us, to see him really happy and to see the quite unique goodness that is his develop, unhampered by the present continual domestic strife. His impression was that the worst crisis for both of them was passed in that unhappy summer two years ago, when you and Johnnie suffered so much, and that from now onwards the good side of each of them will come more and more to the fore, helped by the children who will so soon be of an age to be real companions and helps to them.

I do hope he is right, and that it isn't just the wishful thinking that comes so naturally with two people who have everything in the world to make them the happiest people on earth.

He was most insistent that I ought to keep in much closer touch with them, but though since July I have never once broken my rule of limiting my time in bed to four hours (1–5 a.m.), private letter-writing has simply become completely impossible. I should think there must be nearer a thousand than a hundred unanswered letters on my table.

And it is even more impossible to get away for a few days, as every single one of the twenty hours in each day gets booked up for weeks ahead, and one just can't try to combine another life with this one.

There are, of course, tremendous joys and consolations which make the sacrifice a hundred times worth while. I always feel that Our Lord understated it fantastically when he said that if anyone left father or mother, brother or sister for His sake, he would receive a hundredfold even in this life. There must be a thousand or more families that I have come to love as much as my own.

Do please tell darling Pam that hers will be the very next private letter that I will write, and I, of course, send my warmest love to you all four.

Always your devoted cousin—

Julian

Stonor

22 June 1954

My dearest Noreen,

I am sure telepathy must have told you something of how much you have been living in my thoughts, day and night, for the last six months, but I was in the awful position of not being able to write to you as the postmark would have given the show away and I know how much you and Johnny would have worried, whatever I said.

The work in the parish had suddenly grown like a real avalanche—a new church to hold 1,000 became an urgent necessity for this year and I was kept up till midnight every single night giving instructions to people becoming Catholics and then had to do my accounts, business letters about buildings and schools and get my two hours of monastic prayers said before starting to give Communion again at 5. The result was that during the autumn and early winter I just lay down on top of my bed for 2 or 3 hours and never took my clothes off except to have a bath at 4.30 a.m.—to wake me up!

I had got quite used to that regime and all was going well (except for private letter-writing, which I couldn't even fit in at Christmas—you should have seen the letter I got from Jeanne about it!) until after Christmas we had a long spell of very severe weather. That, of course, made my bad ear inflamed and septic and, as I didn't have time to get it treated, some poisonous germ must have entered through that into my blood stream and gradually poisoned me all over, especially my kidneys.

I didn't realize this and thought I would feel better when the weather got less cold, but one day in February a visiting Dean took one look at me when he opened the door and ordered me straight to bed while he fetched a doctor. For a few days they injected things like penicillin and streptomycin into me, but as they were obviously having no effect except putting me into a sort of coma—they finally moved me to a hospital in Carlisle (in the children's ward, as there was no other bed!), where I remained for the next two months—on a diet of cold water, but with some very precious stuff called aureomycin being injected into me.

While I was there I managed to scribble a note to Jeanne in answer to her ultimatum, and she then told the Abbot that I was ill and between them it was arranged that as soon as I could be moved I should be sent down here to convalesce, which I did, in easy stages, in the middle of April. Since then both she and Sherman and Dr Allan Hartley have been absolutely angelic to me, though terribly strict. Apparently it had left me with a very high blood pressure which meant no physical or mental exertion, so even now I am only allowed to say Mass (in private) twice a week and even letter-writing is strongly discouraged and I have been forbidden by the Abbot even to think about any work before September.

However, all has gone well, and when the doctor came on Friday my blood pressure was normal for the first time and the rest and feeding-up (especially the lovely Stonor creamy milk) has done me so much good that by August he says that I will be fitter than I have ever been since I became a monk 25 years ago.

Naturally you have been in my thoughts the whole time. I am sleeping in your room, my daily walk is up the Ladies' Walk to the hillside before the Warren where I once sat with you years ago; even the fact that only Harriet and Bobby are at home helps the illusion that they are really Pamela and Nicky, though they haven't got quite the spontaneous happiness and affection that makes your two so unique; and on my two visits to the village last week there were the usual flattering references on the part of the older Wats, Shurfields, Heaths, Coombes, Clacks, etc, to the fact that "he is just like Miss Noreen".

I know Johnny will be amused to hear that the Clacks already had their surname four hundred years before the Stonors. While unravelling an old Saxon charter of 774, while this was part of the Kingdom of Mercia, I found that one of the woods at Russell's Water was even then called "Clacc's Woodland", because it belonged to a Saxon called Clacc.

I am determined not to raise the perennial family troubles, but I must just tell you that, though there are squalls, Sherman and Jeanne seem happier together than I ever remember them before. I think it is chiefly because Jeanne has found two interests that absorb all her spare hours to the exclusion of her money-spending visits to London. She spends hours gardening and has made the walled garden at the back really lovely, and she is typing out, with a view to publishing, two volumes of 18th century Stonor letters—and they are such kind, affectionate letters that I think they are having the same softening effect on her as my sleeping pills do on me!

Sherman went through a very bad period when the Bosmore question came up again recently, but he did admit to me one night, which I am sure he would never do to anyone else, least of all to you (out of loyalty to his wife) that it was she who had poisoned his relations with you and had led him to do and say things which he bitterly regretted. But I am afraid he regards any return to normal relations as hopeless because of Jeanne's antipathy or jealousy or whatever it is. It is so maddening, because she couldn't be sweeter or kinder to me, and you will be glad to hear that she has even extracted from Downside a complete new trousseau for me—a new habit, several new suits, including an evening one, and shoes, etc. I felt I must have been such an embarrassment to you at Bockmer two years ago with my one shapeless suit and rather grubby habit, which were eight years old even then.

June 23rd

I was just going to post this and send it off with Pam's this morning when a nice young man arrived to see me having come on a motorcycle 500 miles—he had gone first to Egremont and on being told I was ill at Stonor in <u>Essex</u> had been there next and finally came here. Luckily everything was looking perfect, so I hope it repaid him for his long ride.

But why I am so glad he came is that when he left I found the afternoon post had brought a letter from you with the wonderful news that you will be coming over in September. I do think it is wonderful of you. I am not quite sure yet where I will be at the beginning of September, but I hope it will be at Egremont, even if it is packing up my things and saying goodbyes. Jeanne seems to have some sort of unofficial statement from the Abbot that I will not be going back there. I will, of course, let you know as soon as my plans are definite.

With my fondest love and blessings to you and Johnny and to the two darling children—

always your affectionate
Julian

Downside Abbey
20 July 1954

Dearest Noreen,

Your lovely letter has reached me here just a few hours after I have learned my immediate future from the Abbot, so that you will be the first person I have told.

Alas, it is to be another series of agonizing goodbyes, this time to about two thousand people, as I am being moved from Egremont and sent back to Worth to teach. I will be going there on August 7th, so I will be there when you come to London. I had been feeling utterly heart-broken and miserable, but now I have one wonderful thing to look forward to in seeing all four of you there and it has made me feel much better already.

You were so much in my thoughts yesterday because my mother is staying here at the guest house and yesterday afternoon (a lovely summer's day) I was lent a car and drove her to all the places that I had last visited with you and Johnny—Nunney Castle, Stourton Lake, and Longleat. It seemed only a few days since I was there with you instead of three or four years.

It was three years too since I had seen any of my parishioners at Peasedown and Wellow and so I have had great joys this week as well in re-visiting them all, as I myself had baptized nearly two-hundred out of the two-hundred-fifty of them.

I do know so well what you must have gone through before you finally determined to sell your own piece of Stonor and imitate that most moving gesture of Ruth in the Old Testament. As it was Our Lord who told us that God wanted a wife to leave her father's house and cleave to her husband, I am sure that He blessed you for that act just as much as He does those whom He calls to leave their home to follow Him. In my case, I had no home to leave, but I have come to love Stonor so much now that I can begin to understand what a sacrifice you made. That alone is something that you have accomplished for Him more than I will ever be able to do. And living in the world and yet not being corrupted by its outlook and standards is a daily achievement far harder than anything I have to do who have all the helps of my priesthood and a work which centers round bringing people to know and love Him.

I am so <u>longing</u> to see you all this time. I think each time I long to see you more desperately than the last. My address will be Worth Priory, Crawley, Sussex, and the telephone number is Turner's Hill 246.

With my fondest love to you all—

Julian

Worth Priory
Crawley
Sussex
28 August 1954

Dearest Noreen,

It made such a difference today getting your sweet letter and knowing that I will be seeing you all in only three weeks' time. I have written to the Birch Hotel, Hayward's Heath, which is the most recommended round here, but haven't heard from them yet.

I have to go to Downside for a retreat from September 1st to 10th, but am almost certain that in any case that was when you said you would be in Scotland. (I haven't had time to unpack yet, so I haven't got your letter by me). I hear cousin Charles is taking Thomas to Rome that week.

I don't know whether you have told Sherman of your visit yet, but if there is any difficulty about a hotel anywhere, I am sure he would be able to help now that he is a Director of Trust Houses.

With my fondest love to you all and for weeks now I have been simply living for your visit, without taking any interest in anything else here.

always your affectionate
Julian

as from   Worth Priory
Crawley
Sussex

8 September 1954

My Dearest Noreen,

I hadn't heard a word about the hurricane until I got your letter this evening, as I have been here at Downside for a week making a retreat and haven't seen any newspapers.

Of course you are <u>absolutely</u> <u>right</u> to stay and help people there—you would never have forgiven yourselves if you had come away—and from <u>my</u> point of view the knowledge that you intended coming all that way to see me is just as precious as the memory of the visit would have been afterwards.

The nearer one gets to the end of the journey—and <u>my</u> journey might, of course, end at any time now that I am a heart-case—the shorter it all seems and the nearer that wonderful day seems when all partings will be a dream of the past.

I do want you to know that, if I go before you, I will be even nearer to you than I am now, and that while we are fellow-travellers the few miles of sea between us have long ceased to make any real difference to my vivid picture of you all four, and to my deep, deep love for you and gratitude to God for having let me know you.

I won't bother you with a long letter now, as I know how many calls there will be on your time and your sympathy—it is just to tell you that I am thinking of you more than ever, and <u>thanking</u> you for having wanted to come and then sacrificing that wish to a higher duty—

with my fondest love to you all—
Julian

Worth Priory
Crawley
Sussex

19 September 1954

Darling Noreen,

What <u>wonderful</u> news! I don't think I have ever longed to see you more, and feel a different person already now that I know you are coming.

When I last wrote, I honestly didn't expect to be still here when you got the letter because I had had two days of very high blood pressure which had caused my ankles to get very puffy and swollen, which I had always understood meant that the end was very near in the case of a bad heart, and had certainly seen that happen several times in Egremont.

However, it has passed away completely for the time being and I feel quite well again.

Your suggestion about the chapel has made me absolutely radiantly happy. An awfully nice new priest arrived there about two months ago who is determined to get something done about the appalling state it was getting into, and the new Archbishop, who was appointed at about the same time, is one of the nicest and most charming people who ever lived, so as I am sure it is 'now or never' to save what, as you know, is to me one of the holiest and most sacred spots in England.

And I am sure that all the hundreds and hundreds of Stonor men, women and children who have regarded that chapel as their most precious heritage will all be so happy now that <u>you</u> will be the one to make its survival secure, because, apart from me, I have always felt that you are the only one in this generation of the family who really cares. I am sure they will <u>all</u> (and there really are over 200 who have prayed and who are buried there) be begging Our Lord to pour blessings on you and Johnny and your two children for what you have offered to do, and even though Sherman may not know now which member of the family it was, <u>they</u> will all know, and they are the ones who matter most since they are actually with Our Lord in heaven.

I can't help feeling that in the working of God's Providence there was some real connection between the facts that on the very day when you were writing your wonderful suggestion to me, cousin Charles and Thomas were having a private audience with the Pope (a very unofficial one, as the doctors no longer let him grant them), in which he sent his very special blessing to all the family.

Incidentally he asked for a copy of the book, so we are having one specially bound and inscribed for him.

I was absolutely overwhelmed by the newspapers you sent me of the hurricane. It seems quite unbelievable that people weren't killed by the hundreds, or even thousands.

I am sure you must have found, as I did during air raids and similar experiences during the war, that far outweighing the material damage and the temporary sufferings is the tremendous outpouring of unselfishness, pity and compassion, generosity and goodness of all kinds, of which more and more glimpses gradually come to light. Only God sees into every heart, but I am sure we would no longer wonder why He occasionally presents such things if we could see the goodness and the kindness that it brings out, where before there was perhaps only selfishness. I know there are others like you and Johnny, who use their earthly possessions to give people happiness, but there are so many others who only do so when some urgent need arouses their conscience.

I have one wonderful surprise to show you when you come, which would take too long to tell you about in a letter.

With my deepest love and gratitude to you and Johnny (it is so sweet of him to let you come) and fondest love to Pammy and Nicky.

always your most affectionate
Julian

Worth Priory
25 Oct 1954

Dearest Noreen,

I am writing this at 2 o'clock, thinking of you at Stonor and hoping and praying that they will both be as overjoyed by your visit as I was yesterday—I know I will remember every minute of it as long as I live. I am writing this by my window and, to my joy, I find that I can see the Devil's Dyke as clearly as anything on the skyline, so now every time I glance at the view—which must be about a hundred times a day—my thoughts will fly to you.

It seems so hard to believe that it can be your birthday again tomorrow, because every time I see you you look more radiantly young and lovely than the last and it just seems impossible that you can be growing any older. When that Irish monk you saw in the hall asked me afterwards to repeat my niece's name, as he hadn't caught it, I asked him how old he thought you were, and without a moment's hesitation he said he supposed "about nineteen or twenty". And he is absolutely right.

How lovely to think that that is what you will always look like throughout eternity, since there will be no such thing as old age for our glorified bodies in Heaven.

And even in this short life time seems to become more and more meaningless as one gets older and it is only the momentous things that happen to us and that affect us permanently which seem to live on, while the years in between fade away like forgotten dreams. On October 25th 1936 I was sitting in this very same room looking out at the very same view, and with a robin singing its rather sad little song, just as it is now, and only a few hours before I had just been ordained a priest, with the two Carthusians, and the next morning, which I was so longing for, (your 14th birthday) I would say the words of consecration for the first time and actually hold our Lord in my hands. That is why I particularly wanted to give you that photograph for my birthday present, because I like to feel that God gave you to me as my ordination present. At any rate it will always be the same day of the year that stands alone for both of us—for you because it is the day when you began your life on this earth and for me because it is the day when I began my life as a priest.

You will, of course, be uppermost in my heart when I offer my Mass tomorrow, and though I hope that at 7 o'clock in the morning you will be fast asleep in bed—and like a sleeping child in God's sight despite your thirty-two years—I am sure it won't make any difference to the blessing God will give you. I have always found that you are the easiest person in the world to pray for, because all one has to keep saying to Our Lord is: "Lord, you <u>know</u> how adorable she is, because it was You who made her. Keep her like that <u>always</u>".

I will of course be thinking of you too in all my waking hours on Thursday night and Friday morning, not because I doubt for a moment God's care of you and His knowledge of the love and goodness which led you to brave that journey, but because I will love to think of you as in a way more precious to Him than ever while you thus trust yourself to His arms between the sky and the ocean.

And even though you will be going further and further away from me, you have somehow made the distance seem nothing by this visit, and it will be so lovely to think of you drawing nearer and nearer to Johnny and the children and to your poor mother who alone I feel sorry for, because after not hearing from you on your birthday I am afraid she is bound to know where you are and I can imagine just how anxious she will be. Still, her joy will be all the greater when she is able to hug you in her arms again as tightly and as gratefully as you will <u>your</u> children.

God bless you, Noreen darling, a thousand, thousand times for all the joy you have given me by this visit.

With my fondest love always—

Julian

Worth
11 Nov. 1954

Dearest Noreen,

I have composed so many letters to you in my head and thought of so many things that I wanted to say to you that I can hardly believe that I haven't written you a word since you got back.

But, besides your two lovely letters, the moon did bring me your love too, because both on Saturday night and Sunday night (and again last night) it was so lovely here that I spent a long time each night just gazing across to the Downs and the Dyke and, as always at such times, thinking mostly of you. And last night, while I was looking at it I saw a lovely V-shaped formation of wild ducks or geese flying due west very high up, which I liked to think would be flying over you in the morning, though I expect they were only going to Ireland.

Although at the time it seemed so hard, I suppose I ought really to be glad that Poulton had to be there when we said goodbye; because I loved you so much for having come, and at the same time realized that it must be at least <u>months</u> before you would be so near again (and might always be the last time, as there is always the chance of a stroke from high blood pressure), that I don't know how I could ever have let you go, if we had been alone.

<u>Of course</u> you don't have to be a Catholic to be given a blessing; and nobody could count the hundred thousand times I have asked God to bless you; and sometimes you <u>were</u> kneeling, as in the two chapels here and at Wellow and Downside and Egremont.

Do, <u>please,</u> remember that God's love far transcends any doubts or muddles or hesitations that our little human brains get caught up in while we are on earth. As I remember telling you, He showed it so clearly when he was on earth himself among us by deliberately choosing the Samaritans, the Syro-Phoenician lady, the Roman centurion and the 'publican' (the word doesn't mean what it does with us, but a 'tax-collector' for the Romans, which no Jew was allowed to be) as examples to show us what he meant by real faith, real brotherly love or real humility; and never did he choose a priest or an orthodox Jew as an example, though we know that there were good people among them.

But the incident I am loving most to remember nowadays is the third miracle that Our Lord ever did—only the day after the wedding at Cana. Our Lord never even saw the person for whom he did the miracle and yet he loved him so much that he told his six newly-chosen disciples (who would afterwards be the six chief apostles, including Saint Peter) that he hadn't found faith like this in the whole of Israel. For it was that Roman officer who so admired the Jewish faith that at his own cost he had built them a church in the little lakeside village of Capharnaum, and now shrank from coming and making himself known in person to Our Lord, but had such perfect faith in God's love for his chosen people that although he didn't know yet that Our Lord was God or that he had worked the two miracles twelve miles away the day before, he yet took it for granted that this newly discovered prophet would be able to cure his servant just by praying to God for him from a distance. And so he asked some of his Jewish friends to go for him and make this humble request.

Why, of course, my mind keeps dwelling on <u>that</u> incident so often nowadays is because from heaven our Lord must be loving you and Johnny just as much as He loved that Roman officer. Like him you are restoring a church for other people, not yourselves, to use, and like him you have insisted on keeping in the background yourselves so that your faith and love are known only to God and to the two or three friends through whom you have made your wonderful offering.

It has made me myself even happier than if Sherman and Jeanne had done it; because in their case they would only have been doing their simple duty, like, for instance, Our Lord's host at the supper in Bethany the week before he died. Whereas your gift is just like Mary Magdalen's precious spikenard which she poured out over his head and his feet as her gesture of love, though she wasn't even one of the invited guests at the supper. But, as you can imagine, he loved her more than any of those who were invited and said that wherever the gospel story was told until the end of the world, what she had done that night would be told too.

And so I know that throughout all eternity He will give you and Johnny the same grateful love which He gave Mary Magdalen, and which led him to let her see Him first after the resurrection, before even the apostles. And for all eternity you will rejoice that

84

you so gladly seized this opportunity of pouring out your gift on Him Himself, just as Mary Magdalen did, and not on any of his creatures.

On the purely human level I myself can still hardly believe that I may actually live to see the chapel restored and made beautiful again and a more worthy expression of the family's love and gratitude toward God for all those long centuries during which He had deigned to dwell in their midst and bless them by His presence. It is the one thing in the whole world I have most longed to see, but never thought that I would.

With my deepest, deepest love and gratitude, and begging God to give you all four a foretaste of the blessings he has in store for you in heaven—

your affectionate
Julian

Worth
Christmas Day, 1954

Dearest Noreen,

Never has any Christmas been so much yours as this one.

As you know the recurring refrain running through the whole wonderful story is "The world was made by Him and the world knew Him not; He came unto His own and His own received him not", ending up with that sad aside: "they laid him in a manger, for there was no room for them in the inn".

It is because of that sad refrain that where you get really poor people who realize what a blessing it is just to have somewhere to live, as in the west of Ireland or Brittany, every little cottage leaves the door ajar on Christmas night, with a lamp or candle burning in the window, to show that they would gladly have given their home to his mother that night.

For those who are richer and more educated, such a make-believe gesture would obviously be forced and artificial; but this year you and Johnny have really and truly and at very great cost quite literally furnished for him the most fitting home within your power in the spot where you knew that he had been loved and worshipped by all your family for century after century and where I now feel quite certain he will be loved and worshipped again as a result of your wonderful gesture.

Already, before they knew of this marvellous crowning gift, the rest of the family have at last begun to show that longing to do something for the Chapel that had been so sadly lacking before. Sherman has already had the sacristy roof mended and fitted the Chapel with electric light at his own expense; Jeanne organized a big Jumble Sale for the Chapel at the end of October; and Charles has been giving lantern-slide lectures on the Himalayas at fifteen guineas a time—all the proceeds to go to the Chapel. So I really do feel that it will be with real love for Our Lord and the desire to revive the family's former magnificent devotion to him that they will receive your wonderful gift this Christmas and lay it at his feet. I hope that perhaps it will reach Sherman by the Epiphany so that it can be offered in spirit with the gifts brought by the Magi.

But my greatest joy of all, as you can imagine, is to know that Our Lord himself knows perfectly well that it is <u>you</u> who have given him this home and just as quietly and unobtrusively as his mother and Saint Joseph would have done. He never tired of telling us to give in secret like that so only He, who sees our most secret thoughts, knows—and knows that it is given to <u>Him</u> only. I am sure <u>you</u> must remind Him in so many ways of his own mother; physically she must have been very dark-haired and dark-eyed and we know from the image of her Son's face on the shroud that she must have had an oval-shaped face and high forehead just like yours; but, much more lovely than that, I am sure there is a great deal in common in your two souls—the same incapability of hurting anyone or anything and the same rare and precious gift of being able to give a love that has all the intensity and yet all the purity of a child's, just like Pamy's or Nicky's.

Your absolutely lovely Christmas letter was so completely <u>you</u> that I have been feeling just as happy every time I read it as if you were still staying at East Grinstead and I were going to be seeing you again any minute. I loved you for your deliciously honest confession about the difficult words to spell, but I would <u>far</u> rather you spelt them in your own way, which I am sure would be much better than the complicated ways the learned professors have thought out!

Your saying that you have 46 letters of mine though rather terrifying, is also rather a relief; because I always feel I have been so horribly ungrateful in often leaving you waiting so long for an answer, and my impression was that I had probably only written one to every two or three of yours. But actually I can't have been quite so bad as I thought. For I only have 38 of yours—my most precious possessions in the world—but when I went to Caldey (as I hoped, for life) I had to destroy all the ones I had received till then.

It was very clever of you to quote my own words against me, because it is certainly true that if I had been allowed to stay on Caldey I would never have known any of the myriad joys I afterwards discovered at Peasedown and Wellow and then, even more, at Egremont, and, most of all, during <u>your</u> visits to those places and to Bockmer and here; so perhaps one day I will see God's plan behind this last uprooting. The Abbot has asked me to go to Downside for a week on January 7th, so I am hoping then to broach the subject of America!

It would be so <u>wonderful</u> to have a picture of you in your own setting to carry in my mind for ever afterwards. Curiously enough it never seems to be the highlights of your visits that come most spontaneously into my mind, but pictures of you in between times—in your last visit it is nearly always the memory of you while we were just driving along the country lanes that afternoon that comes first, and then of you having dinner that night in that hotel in Crawley; but all the other memories soon come flooding in afterwards, and I don't think I will ever forget a single moment.

My one and only regret is that my greatest joy of all here only came too late for you to see her, as you would have absolutely <u>adored</u> her, just as much as I do. She is a three-year-old thoroughbred mare: "Honeymoon" by "Chaotic" out of "No Honey"—beautifully bred (11 out of her 14 immediate sires were Derby winners and the 'Honey' mares are world-famous); she is just as intelligent as a human being, and we fell in love with each other at first sight—just as I did when I first saw you! She has the most gentle, affectionate character I have ever known in any horse—her welcome in the few minutes that I can slip up to see her every day is almost embarrassing—whinnying and scraping with her forefoot and nodding her head up and down, followed by about four kisses as soon as I get within range; and if I take her out to get some fresh grass she follows me like a dog, or rather dances along beside me, without any need even for a head-collar; and on the two days a week when I have a whole hour I either go for a ride on her—she almost reads one's thoughts when being ridden and knows all her dressage backwards—or else turn her loose to exercise herself in the indoor school, where she knows just what is wanted—dancing and bucking and standing on her hind legs, just like a very graceful circus horse, and cantering up after each buck or prance to give me a kiss; yet the moment you put a head collar on (she almost puts it on herself, she is so co-operative) she is as proud and dignified as a show hack at Richmond. She is away during the holidays, as she has been given to Miss Moore, but I had a lovely Christmas card from her, dictated to Miss Moore!, telling me all about her adventures! As soon as I have got a photograph of her, I will of course send you one.

How lovely your meeting the Darrell-Rews—I forget whether I ever told you the wonderful story of how their marriage came right almost the day after Dorothy became a Catholic—her previous husband—who had become a sort of dipsomaniac—dying very suddenly the very next day, just after Patrick and Dorothy had accepted the agonizing obligation of having to separate. I know you will give them both my love when you see them again, and also Patrick Higgins, and with all the love in my heart to you and Johnny and Pamy and Nicky and almost hourly blessings—

always your affectionate

Julian

Worth Priory
Crawley
Sussex

28.4.55

Dearest Noreen,

I am <u>determined</u> to write to you tonight even if I don't go to
bed at all; because a new 3 month term has just begun and with
all the teaching to prepare and correct and an unending stream
of guests and visitors to look after I don't know when I will get
another opportunity.

I too am so sorry that your lovely thought for the Chapel has
taken so long to bear fruit; though in the end it will make Sherman just as happy, whenever it comes, and of course Our Lord
loved you for it and took it as done the moment the thought
came into your heart, just as I did.

I expect the trouble is that the new Archbishop, who is a charming person, has been desperately busy, as it is a huge industrial
diocese covering the whole of the Midlands, with a quarter of a
million Catholics and 350 churches, of which Stonor is probably
the smallest, even though it is the oldest. But I do hope he will
have been there by now and that the restoration will be able to
take place this summer.

Like you, I haven't heard a word from Jeanne since I left in July,
or from the children, though I have written two or three times. I
don't think she will ever really forgive me for that wretched night
when I thought I was no longer wanted, and fled. But I have had
two very nice and kind letters from Sherman.

I am afraid the chances of my being able to accept your wonderful invitation this year have grown so remote that I no longer
think of it even as a possibility. Although the school holidays in
the summer last eight weeks, for the monks they only last six
and a half, owing to a retreat and a gathering at Downside in
the second week of September, and they have to be so arranged
that there are always at least half a dozen monks here to keep
all the services in church going. And in any case I haven't had
a moment to prepare any retreats or sermons, without which it
wouldn't be fair for me to come. So I am hoping to slip away to

the Cumberland hills for two or three weeks in August and there prepare a series of retreats, so that I would have them ready if by any luck I find myself no longer teaching next year.

Darling Pam's school sounds absolutely lovely. I have always been fascinated by everything I have ever read about Virginia and the deep south, and feel that in many ways it must be almost more English than the present-day England is, and yet with a tremendous character of its own. I do hope she will love it and that it will deepen her love for America tremendously.

It will be so wonderful if you can come over to England again when you have left her there. But if you do come I am sure you will never get any further than Honeymoon's box—she is so adorable and I know will lose her heart to you at first sight. She only went away for the Christmas holidays, but these holidays she was left in my charge and has been so sweet. She hears my steps at an incredible distance and starts whinnying and by the time I reach the box is pawing the ground with impatience to be petted.

The news from Cumberland continues to be wonderful. The two young priests who are there have both been thrilled by the goodness of the people. 880 out of 1,000 came to Mass at Easter, which must be very nearly all, as the rest would be babies or very old and unable to get out. And they are so faithful about writing, even though I am hardly ever able to answer. I haven't answered most of their Christmas letters yet and now I have 118 more Easter letters and cards to answer.

But I try not to think of them too much, as it makes me feel so restive here, now that I am absolutely fit again. This term I have nothing to teach but elementary Latin and Greek grammar to beginners, which are such very uninspiring subjects.

With my fondest love to you all four—
always your affectionate
Julian

Worth Priory
Crawley
Sussex

13 May 1955

Dearest Noreen,

I received the enclosed very happy letter this morning from Sherman and so I must send it straightaway to you to whom it really belongs and add once more my own heartfelt thanks for the thing that has meant most to me of anything that could have happened in the world. And, of course, the fact that it is you who have done it has made it a million times more precious to me.

In the end, I think the timing of it has made it an even greater consolation for Sherman than if he had known at Christmas, because, although he doesn't say anything about it in his letter (I expect, out of kindness to me), I learnt in a letter two days ago from those friends of mine at Kimble Farm that he has a great deal of land up for sale and is feeling it very much.

Don't be alarmed by the rumours he had heard about me. I am really very much better and happier this term. The Headmaster has been away in hospital for a month or two, and is not coming back this term, and his substitute has halved the number of my classes and given me subjects that I find easier, such as history and Latin. And so I can find an hour or two most days to help a bit, unofficially, with Honeymoon and the ponies.

I still haven't heard whether I will be allowed away at all in August, but my mother is trying to get permission to take me to Ireland for a month. She herself is not allowed more than a few days in England owing to money regulations.

With my fondest love to you all four, and thank you again, Noreen, with <u>all</u> my heart for the deepest earthly joy you could have given me.

Always your most affectionate
Julian

Worth Priory
1 August 1955

My dearest, dearest, Noreen,

I have no less than five absolutely lovely letters of yours which I have never answered; but today is the first day of my official holiday—for we don't have guests to stay during the month of August, so, unless any stray visitors arrive to be shown round, I am hoping to be able to spend the next hour or two writing to you—or just thinking about you and loving you, as I usually do when I start writing.

Sherman keeps writing very happily about the Chapel, and it has been the means of bringing him into really friendly relations with the saintly Archbishop, so I am sure that is the first of many, many, blessings with which God will repay your great generosity.

I am so sorry myself that Evelyn Waugh's appeal seems to emphasize the Catholic v. Protestant aspect of the past three centuries rather than the thousand years before when we were all Catholics; but at least God, when He looks down from heaven, knows that the greatest benefactor of all to the restoration of the Chapel is one whose heart is big enough to bridge the gulf.

I hear Charles is writing a pamphlet on the Chapel's history and also a book about the Himalayas, but he is an even worse letter-writer than I am and I haven't heard from him for a year. I rather think Jeanne has never forgiven me for the night I ran away because although I have written to her several times during the last year she has never answered, whereas she used to write much more often than Sherman.

I loved the idea of Nicky's camp in Maine and how glad you must be now that you had the strength to let him go. I am sure it will have done him a world of good spiritually and physically to be on his own like that; but it must be the hardest thing a mother ever has to do to begin that weaning process.

When darling Pam goes down to Virginia do, please, get hold of an illustrated catalogue of the school for me, so that I can picture her. I have a lovely clear picture of Merrymount in my mind, so I love your being there for that reason, but most of all because I always feel you are happier there than anywhere else.

It will be <u>wonderful</u> if we are able to spend a month together somewhere next summer. There are all kinds of ideas I am toying with already: that lovely farm at the foot of the Great Gable in Cumberland where I stayed on our riding tour; the island of Barra in the Hebrides; Lulworth; or somewhere in the Cotswolds. I am <u>hoping</u> to have a fortnight in Cumberland this month, but it is not at all certain. I had to cancel my Irish plans.

Poor darling Honeymoon had to be destroyed a fortnight ago. She fell in her box and broke one of her hind legs at the hip. The worst of it was that it was a Sunday, and it was three hours before we could get anyone to come and put her out of her pain, and every time I left her to go and telephone she struggled to come after me. I still get haunted by it all night long, as she was the most affectionate creature that ever lived; there was nothing but love in her heart.

Did you know that the supreme champion hack this year at Richmond, the White City, etc, is a son of your Cadogan Memory. He has been produced and shown by Harry Tatlow too, though his owner is a Colonel Coote of Exeter. His name is Royal Command. I will try and find a photo of him to send you.

With my fondest love to Johnny, and to Pamy and Nicky, and <u>longing</u> to see you next August—

your affectionate
Julian

Worth

12.9.55

Dearest Noreen,

Just a hurried line to thank you for your lovely letter for my birthday, and to tell you that I was suddenly sent for to Downside this weekend and was told to report the day after tomorrow as the second curate in our one remaining city parish, in the Liverpool docks. My address will henceforth be

St. Mary's, Highfield St, Liverpool, 3

It will be a strange experience for me living for the very first time in my life in a city, without any birds or animals or even a tree. The church is new and rather nice, but the house is the darkest and dingiest I have ever seen (I called in there once on my way down from Cumberland) and right up against the main line station. However, the people are said to be really wonderful, and I will be far happier, I am sure, doing parish work than trying so unsuccessfully to teach noisy small boys.

I will write and tell you more about it when I have settled in; meanwhile my heartfelt congratulations to Nicky on having done so marvelously at camp, and my equally heartfelt good wishes to Pam on the 25th. I do hope she won't find the parting too hard—and my fondest, fondest, love to you all four—   Julian

St Mary's
Highfield St
Liverpool 3

4 Oct. 1955

Dearest Noreen,

I am afraid this won't be in time to wish Johnny a very, very, happy birthday on Thursday—still, as he is far and away the luckiest person in the whole world, having <u>you</u>, it seems almost superfluous to wish him happiness, and I know he knows how much I love and admire him (he is the only person I know whose character and goodness I really feel to be worthy of you) and that I will be thinking of him all day on Thursday.

I do hope you aren't all missing Pam too terribly and that the darling child herself isn't feeling too homesick. I haven't been able to get her out of my mind since the 25th—not that I wanted to!—but I hope that by now she will have begun to make real friends with the others and will be her usual radiantly happy self.

It is strange how things work out, but actually I am a thousand, thousand, times happier here than I was at Worth—with its lovely setting, its horses and ponies, and so much else. Here there is nothing but almost unbelievable squalor—it is said to be the dirtiest city in the world, and we are situated between a railway station and a tannery—and the only animals are the fleas and other small creatures with which every room abounds—and yet I am as happy as the day is long and only wish that each one was a thousand times longer.

I suppose it was because I couldn't put my heart into teaching Latin and Greek grammar, at which I knew I was so bad—and couldn't feel in those surroundings that I had in any way left everything to follow our Lord in the way He meant; whereas here one is a priest and nothing but a priest from the moment one gets up until the moment one goes to bed.

There are two other priests in the house, who have both been here since before the war, and both far kinder and nicer than the Prior who made my life such a misery at Worth—I won't tell you what he did, because I don't think you would ever believe me.

The actual pier-head is in our parish, and, though I haven't seen one yet, I believe quite a lot of liners leave there for Canada and the States and arrive from there. If so, it will make you seem only just out of sight.

With my <u>fondest</u> love to you all three,

from
Julian

St Mary's

Highfield St

Liverpool, 3

19 Oct. 1955

Dearest Noreen,

Alas, I am single-handed this week, as one of the priests has gone off to Palestine for three weeks and the other to make a retreat at Downside; so I hardly know what to do next, I am so busy.

But I must at least send you my deepest, deepest, love for Wednesday, when you will be in my thoughts all day long. You really seem quite close now, because the actual landing-stages are in this parish and almost every day I see carriers coming from, or going to, New York.

I am not minding the dirt and squalor and the absence of grass and trees and birds, etc, nearly as much as I thought I would. In fact I am so busy that I have hardly missed them at all; and every day brings new miracles of grace which more than make up for everything else. I think our Lord must be deliberately spoiling me to make up for the surroundings.

I _do_ hope darling Pam has really settled down happily. When you next write could you please send me her address. And if sometime you are able to get hold of an illustrated booklet advertising the school, I would love to have a picture of it in my mind. I have always been fascinated by everything I have ever read about Virginia—with its English parks and its horses.

I had a letter from Sherman, a week or two ago, sounding _really_ happy about the work that is going on in the Chapel. I want to wait until I can go with you before I see what he has been able to have done.

With my fondest love to you both and to Nicky—and a very, very, special blessing to you on Wednesday—

your devoted   Julian

St Mary's
Highfield St
Liverpool, 3

10 Dec. 1955

Dearest Noreen,

I must get my Christmas wishes to you off before the rush starts, as it will be very hard to snatch a few minutes in the next fortnight.

How awful for you about Merrymount, but I do think you were very wise and I am so glad you both found the strength of mind to do it. And the beach house in Florida sounds absolutely enchanting—to read about such warmth and sunshine on a December day in Liverpool, which is so dark and wet and foggy that we have had the lights on all day, makes it seem like fairyland. I will love thinking of you all there after the 27th.

Thank you very much for sending me the Foxcroft Catalog. All schools look very chilling and impersonal in those sort of posed photographs, especially when one doesn't know the children, and I am sure it would be much more comforting for the mothers if they published an album of informal snapshots of the children really enjoying themselves, taken when they weren't looking.

But it is lovely to know that Pam is so happy there, and I am so glad you chose such an 'English'-looking school, deep in the south, with lovely country and horses to ride, and such a much bigger variety of activities than you get in schools over here. I particularly liked the idea of the bigger ones going to the baby clinic in Middleburg and teaching the small children in the public school there, and going to Washington for concerts and art exhibitions.

If I am still here at the end of June, I might really be able to join you on your trip for a bit, but don't dare think too much about it until nearer the time. My mother, who has always longed to meet you, has set her heart on my visiting Assisi with her in the early summer and perhaps Florence and Siena as well, which are quite near. So perhaps we could all meet there.

I don't suppose you will really enjoy this book very much, but I thought you ought to have a copy. Having spent all his life with so many hundreds of horses, and also with so many hundreds of different people, he has missed the joy of a really deep love and affection, whether for horses or people, as individuals. I was very conscious of the same thing when I spent a day with Cynthia Haydon last summer.

My fondest love to you all and frequent visits in my thoughts, at Christmas itself when you are in New York, but, still more, when you are all alone together in Florida—

your affectionate
Julian

St. Mary's
Highfield Street
Liverpool
19 Dec 1955

Dearest Noreen,

I am trying hard to imagine you all in the warmth and sunshine of Florida, but it takes a tremendous lot of imagination, because here we have had the most prolonged fog on record. We haven't seen the sky since October and by 3.30 in the afternoon it is literally pitch dark, and you can taste the soot in the air even in the house. And, to add to our discomfort, the parish priest hasn't turned the heating on in the church yet, so that it is exactly like a refrigerator.

But physical hardships don't worry me at all. What I find far harder, as I know you do, is the pressure of modern life which never allows us any real peace or quiet. Since I started this letter I have had a least seven major interruptions and it is already twenty-four hours later and a Saturday morning, so as I won't have another chance till Monday morning (I have to give an address on Christian-Jewish relations on Sunday evening to about 500 people, including many Jews, so it will take me all my nights preparing it) I think I had better send it as it is, to make sure it gets to you in time.

As you know, it brings my very deepest love to all four of you, and there is nobody I will be thinking of more often all through Christmastime.

Bless you all—now and always—
Julian

St Mary's

Highfield Street

Liverpool, 3

29 Dec. 1955

My dearest Noreen,

You couldn't have given me anything more precious. As you know, I have always <u>longed</u> for a really good photograph of you, but you always said there never had been one. But this one, though it doesn't make you quite as lovely as you are in real life, is honestly good enough to make me feel you are actually in the room whenever I look at it. So, of course, it will always be on my desk right before my eyes.

I thought it was awfully sweet of Pam too, chiefly because it gives her such a look of you. But, if it is really like she is now, she has changed tremendously since Bockmer days, and I see what you mean about her being thinner since she has been away at school.

I am so thrilled that you have the same receptiveness to telepathy as I have. I always felt sure that you had. With me it is almost a joke and it is very seldom that a day goes by without at least one striking example of it. Today, for instance, two people have said as soon as I rang them up: "I was just on my way to the hall to ring <u>you</u> up" in one case, and in the other: "I was just in the middle of writing a letter about you when the bell rang". They always think it is a wonderful coincidence, but it happens to me so many times a week that I always take it for granted now. But, of course, I am <u>tremendously</u> grateful for the gift, when it is the knowledge that <u>you</u> are thinking of me.

Distance doesn't seem to make the slightest difference to the clearness of the perception. I remember one Old Downside boy who was out in the forests of Burma noticing that although we only wrote to each other about once or twice a year (and not at Christmas) that when they arrived, a month or so later, our letters <u>always</u> proved to have been written on the same day. And my mother always gets furious, because our letters invariably seem to cross each other; as when she is writing to me I know she is thinking of me and, if I am able to, I sit down and write to her. It is the same with my younger sister, Molly.

102

One lovely thing which I would never have known otherwise came out of your sweet letter to me about Liverpool—that you yourself somehow manage to find time to work for two hospitals. It has made me so happy. Actually I myself only look after one of our two hospitals—the eye one.

As you said they would, the people here seem to become more and more loveable every day, and the days seem all too short. You would love my latest addition to my flock. A really first-class international circus has come into my district of the parish for the next six weeks—a number of them are booked to go on to Bertram Mills for three years when they leave here—they are all Catholics, except one family, and are so good and kind. They insist on my visiting them all in their caravans and are so pleased if I can come in and watch them practising, and they are all so wonderfully kind to their animals—I will tell you all about them in the summer. There are five elephants, a lion and four lionesses, ten horses, including six Arab stallions, and six adorable little black ponies. All the animals adore doing their acts and if one of them has a cold or anything and isn't allowed in, it gets miserable when it recognizes its own tune being played by the orchestra. The Austrian girl who trains the lions is only nineteen, but can do anything with them.

I do hope you are having a wonderful time in Florida to make up for the terribly cold weather in New York which I read about.

With my fondest love to you all, and hoping that you will all four have the happiest year you have ever had so far; I know I will, because I already feel certain that we will be able to spend two or three weeks together...

with a big, big blessing—
Julian

LETTERS
1956–62

St Mary's
Highfield St
Liverpool, 3

23 Feb. 1956

Dearest Noreen,

It must have been telepathy your both wanting to go to Ireland. Since being here and meeting Irish friends almost every day going or coming between Ireland and England I have been longing more and more to revisit it and was wondering whether you and Johnny would be hurt if I suggested our visiting the West of Ireland together instead of Italy. So you can imagine how thrilled I was when I read your letter this morning.

The only difficulty is going to be dates. I have now been told that I can only take my holiday between July 2nd and July 28th.

So what I am going to suggest is that I spend my first week in Cumberland while you are at Beaulieu, and that then we cross over together about July 10th or 11th for a fortnight. You could then go to Scotland for the <u>beginning</u> of August (the nicest time there, and also a very easy crossing from the north of Ireland—the same as from Dover to Calais), and then spend your last month on the continent, visiting Molly, etc, and ending up at Cherbourg on September 6th.

I am <u>longing</u> for you to see Connemara and Mayo, and I have just made the most wonderful discovery about my own great-grandmother, my mother's grandmother. I think I once told you about her being a famous beauty; but we always thought that she was just a village girl, but I have now discovered that she came from Ballynalachan Castle on the wildest part of the Atlantic coast exactly opposite the famous Aran Islands in Galway Bay and that she was quite unique in Ireland because she was descended in direct male line from seventeen kings, including the greatest of all the Irish kings, Brian Boru (950–1020). So I am longing to see this romantic-sounding castle.

If you think there is any chance of our being able to do all this together, will you let me know as soon as you can, and I will start making inquiries about hotels, etc, which will be quite easy here, as this is the gateway into Ireland.

I mustn't write more now as I have to seize any odd moments I can get during the day to prepare the sermons on the enclosed card, as they are for the whole of Liverpool and collect hundreds of people, and preaching is not my strong point at all. So please remember me <u>specially</u> in your prayers during that week.

With my fondest love to you all—and longing for your visit more than for anything else in the whole world—

Julian

St Mary's
Highfield Street
Liverpool, 3

6 May 1956

Noreen darling—you were absolutely <u>inspired</u> to find that article in Vogue. Count Cyril McCormack was in the same House as me at Downside (and I <u>loved</u> his father's singing), so as he is the great authority on visits to Ireland <u>and</u> the chief person from whom people hire cars, I thought the best thing was to put the whole thing in his hands, and have asked him to correspond with you direct by air.

I have given him the <u>dates</u> and all the other facts (including the bathroom!) and have told him the particular places I wanted to show you; and have told him that Dromoland Castle would be the most perfect of all in every way, and only six miles from Shannon Airport, which would be easy for you. It is the ancestral home of the O'Briens, who still live there, but run it as a hotel, and in the exact centre of all the places I want you to see—Adare, the Cliffs of Moher, the Aran Islands in Galway Bay, Galway, Connemara and Croaghpatrick.

It is <u>so</u> sweet of you both to make this possible—and never in my life have I longed for anything so much. Please thank Johnny very, very, much for me. If I have to swim and walk there from Liverpool, I will be waiting at Shannon when your plane touches down.

With my fondest, fondest love and <u>longing</u> to see you—

Julian

St. Mary's Priory
Highfield Street
Liverpool, 3.
12 August 1956

My dearest Noreen,

I do hope I haven't been keeping you in suspense too long for you to make all your arrangements. But it was only late last night that I was able to find out what I would be able to do.

As soon as I got back from my three days with Molly, I was suddenly sent off to supply on another parish in North Lancashire where the priest was ill and only got back here this week-end—to find that the parish priest here has gone to Ireland and won't be back till the 23rd—that a German monk who has been supplying here has to go back tomorrow, and only late last night was I able to borrow a young monk from Ealing to help us out till the 23rd. But he is _very_ young—only just ordained—and has never been on a parish, so I simply can't leave him on his own. So I really can't even come to Cumberland for the inside of a day (the journey takes 5 hours by train, though only 2 by car).

Failing any unexpected crisis, I have kept the whole of Friday free from 1 o'clock onwards, and Saturday between 1.30 and 7.30. And on Sunday morning I am doing the 9 o'clock and 10 o'clock Masses; so perhaps during the second one you could go to a service in the _lovely_ Anglican cathedral?

I do hope you have been having a lovely time—though I am sure nothing can have been as lovely as Connemara—

with all my love—
Julian

P. S. The hotel in Seascale was called "The Scawfell". Just in case they can't put you up—other good ones in Cumberland are

"The Pheasant", Bassenthwaite

"The Bower House", Eskdale

"The Fish Hotel", Buttermere,

  or, best of all,

"The Scalehill", Loweswater

St Mary's
Highfield Street
Liverpool, 3

18 August 1956

Dearest Noreen,

If it wasn't for the sad reason for it and the knowledge of poor Johnny's pain, I think I would almost be glad that you didn't come to Liverpool after all. It has been pouring with rain since yesterday morning without stopping and looks as if it is going on right through the week-end; and, what would have made it even worse, the parish priest hasn't come back yet, so that I have had to do all the evening confessions and only had from 2 till 6 free.

I do hope Johnny isn't in very great pain. Some breaks can be very, very painful. But when I think how angelically you will be nursing him, I confess I go green with envy and wish him long weeks of this peaceful existence, with his family all round him and, I hope, not too many visitors.

I have naturally been toying with the idea of becoming one of the visitors myself, even though it would have to be a fleeting visit in the night; but now there really does seem to be a chance that I may be able to visit London officially, even if only passing through. Because I heard yesterday morning that the chaplain immediately below me on the Reserve list had just received his notice of re-call because of the Suez crisis; so, though I find it very hard to believe (and harder still to justify) that they will go to war over this incident, I may get called up for a time and so will probably pass through London.

I can't remember what address for me the War Office have, but I am more or less expecting the notice to reach me on Monday or Tuesday.

Again and again and again I find my thoughts going back to those heavenly days in Ireland. More than anywhere I have ever been to it reminded me of Caldey, especially the little cemetery on the island of Lettermullen where we watched the funeral.

While you are in London I do hope you will be able to arrange the purchase of your little house at Ballynalachan with the breath-taking view, and also that you will be able to find a really true-to-life painting of Connemara to take back to America with you.

I am afraid only one of my films came out—I am enclosing copies, as I had two done of each—and I am also enclosing a little medal for Rose. I do wish there was sometimes something that I could give to you and Johnny and to the children; but you know that you have a love such as I never have and never could feel for anyone else on earth. Each of you in your own way, and all of you in your wonderful happiness together, are the nearest I can imagine to what people will be like in heaven.

With my fondest love to you all four, and I am sure that not even your mother can think of you more often than I do.

Bless you always—
Julian

St Mary's
Highfield St
Liverpool 3

24 August

Dearest Noreen—

For once my luck deserted me yesterday and I got to the Ritz just five minutes after you had all left for Cornwall. Still, it was <u>wonderful</u> to know that Johnny was well enough to undertake the journey, and of course the thought of your visit here on my birthday has made me deliriously happy.

I was on my way to a Requiem Mass for Sir John Reynolds—a very old friend of mine—and had called in at Stonor for an hour the evening before. Unfortunately I just missed Sherman, and Harriet and Charles but Jeanne and the other children were really very nice.

An Irish Guards Colonel, another great friend of Jack Reynolds, had met me in Oxford and was driving me down to his house at Southampton for the night and I had been hoping to spend the rest of yesterday with you all; as I hadn't then received your letter. But I am <u>so</u> glad that you have all been able to see Molly, and only hope the journey wasn't too much of an agony for poor Johnny.

The parish priest got back yesterday, but is off again on Monday, so I will be on full duty on the 28th, I am afraid, but Tuesday is nearly always the least busy day of the week.

Thank you very, very much for such a sweet thought. With my fondest love to you all—

Julian

St Mary's
Highfield St
Liverpool, 3

Friday morning

My dearest Noreen,

I will never forget my last picture of you. I don't think you could see it, but your carriage in the train was framed in a most lovely bright rainbow. It seemed to set the most wonderful seal on the happiness you brought with you.

I am afraid my only hope of seeing you all again before you go now rests on my being called back to the army for a spell—as I am going to be single-handed here until the end of next week. The other curate went off to Lourdes this morning, till next Friday, and for the weekend I am having to depend on a secular priest who is coming up from London, as the parish priest is going to Downside for the Chapter.

I rang Colonel Philpotts to tell him that I wouldn't be able to come and he suggested, very charmingly, that it would be far happier for me to be at the bottom of his lawn to wave to you next time you are coming to England rather than the sadness of seeing you sail away.

But it is sad not seeing Johnny again and the two darling children and not having been able to kiss you goodbye owing to the suddenness of your parting!

But I love Pam and Nicky's cards. Pam sent me a sweet one as well as the one with the nice smudge on it, (which somehow makes her feel much more near), and, of course, I am longing to be sent the perfect person or persons on whom to do the good which you and Johnny have so sweetly put in my power. I think it is just possible that it may enable Josie Doyle to go to Lourdes.

I do hope your visit to Stonor will be a really happy one in spite of everything. I always feel that when you are there all the many many Stonors from the past who are now in heaven are looking down on you and loving you—and now thanking you for all you have done.

Bless you always—and thank you both again and again and again for the hundreds of most wonderful memories that those

wonderful eight days in Ireland have given me—and now for giving even Liverpool its associations with you. (I will never be able to go to the Cathedral again without feeling you beside me)—
always your devoted
Julian

St Mary's

Highfield St

Liverpool, 3

23 Oct. 1956

Dearest Noreen,

Thank you so much for your lovely letter, though it was dreadful to hear that Johnny had had to have his arm re-broken and re-set. I do hope all this long period of pain and discomfort hasn't pulled down his general health. And I remember when I broke mine as a child that one of the worst things was exercising it afterwards to bring it back to normal use. Poor Johnny! I do feel so much for him. And your back has set me worrying again like your mother, because all the nerves travel up one's spine and anything wrong there can be so painful.

I am afraid I haven't had a moment to go down to the Pier Head again since I went there with you, but every time I go out of the house I see the Cathedral which always floods my mind with memories of you.

I had a sweet letter from Pam the other day, which I am hoping to answer this evening, but I must get this one off to you first to be in time to bring all my love and prayers to you for Friday—I will literally be thinking of you from the moment I get up till I go to bed.

Bless you both ever so much—

Julian

St Mary's
Liverpool
6.11.56

My dearest Noreen,

I must get a few lines across the Atlantic to you both today, with a fervent prayer that whoever your President is to be, he will be given the strength he will need as the one hope left for the civilized world.

Everyone over here feels so sick with shame and misery at what Eden has done, but there seems to be no way of getting rid of him. I keep thinking of the dear Syechenyis and the agony they must have been going through. I do hope you have both been with them some of the time to comfort them by your goodness, as only you two could—Everybody over here feels that if we hadn't gone back to the law of the jungle the Russians would never have dared to go back there like they did.

I don't know whether they have published in America the awful leaflets we have been dropping on Egypt, threatening to bomb their wives, their children, their mothers and all that they have if they don't give up Nasser. It is all so horrible.

If I get called back to the army, which might happen any day, I feel I couldn't possibly give it my moral support as a Chaplain because it is only permitted to kill in self-defence—so I suppose I will go to prison as a conscientious objector.

At any rate, wherever I am even if it is only the depressing streets of Liverpool—I have one joy that nobody can ever take from me—my many, many, memories of the one <u>perfect</u> family I have ever known.

With my fondest, deepest, love to you all four—

Julian

St Mary's
Liverpool
Christmas Eve

Dearest Noreen—

All your letters arrived today, including a really <u>lovely</u> card from darling Pam, which sent my hopes rocketing up for a few moments when I saw it had a Belgian stamp on it.

I myself am feeling rather forlorn this Christmas, because none of my own cards will reach anybody in time for Christmas, and yours (which, of course, matters to me most) probably not till the Epiphany, as I don't know your address in Florida.

For the last fortnight or so I have been working at higher pressure than ever before in my life, but it has all been intermingled with such a fantastic <u>series</u> of the most wonderful experiences (one of them, I think, really miraculous)—most of them deaths, including, at last, my dear little Josie, but some of them quite amazing conversions—that it has had a wonderfully calming effect on me. Although one thing follows another in an unending stream for 19 or 20 hours a day, and half the things completely unexpected and unplanned, God's timing of them has been so unbelievably accurate (to the very minute in almost every case) that it has brought a great sense of peace and of certainty as to God's providence. The only thing which has suffered has been my Christmas mail.

I wish I could tell you about some of the things, but it would take too long, so I will wait till I see you; because I must try and write as many letters as I can tonight.

I felt rather guilty about my last depressed letter written when Eden seemed bent on plunging us into another world war; but, thank heaven, we very soon began shifting back on to the side of law and order; though, alas!, it completely sapped our moral strength, just when Hungary needed all our moral support.

There was a horrid period when the guilty people here tried to pin the blame on America, but the verdict of history will obviously be that America upheld the western ideals <u>magnificently</u> throughout.

Your darling Pam wrote me a sweet letter from school last term, and this term I am <u>determined</u> to write her one—and Nicky too.

Do please thank them both for their lovely cards. It was so like them to take such trouble that their greetings should reach me over all those thousands of miles that separate us...

With my fondest love and blessings to you all four, and I will be thinking of you so often during these next days at Newport, in New York and in Florida—

Julian

St Mary's
Highfield Street
Liverpool, 3

23 May 1957

Dearest Noreen,

It was so like you both to think of a visit to Liverpool the very day you decided about Paris. You really are <u>so</u> true and loyal in your affection that it absolutely hurts—though a <u>lovely</u> kind of pain!

If you can manage to fit it in—but of course I will under-stand if you can't—I will be here all through the summer. If I do have a holiday this year, it won't be before September. Fr. Julian Stead from Portsmouth Priory is coming here on his way back to America for good after finishing his Doctorate in Rome, but it will be a bit after you. He is arriving on July 11th and sailing from here on the 13th.

If you do manage it—I expect you will!!—I know a much nicer hotel for you to stay. The Dunalleys discovered it—the people we had supper with at Silvermines—they have been over twice in the last few months (and each time we talked till exactly midnight). It is called the Blundellsands Hotel—is most comfortable and with far better food than the Liverpool hotels, but, above all, is on the sea, just clear of Liverpool and its smoke, and yet is only 15 min-utes from my door by electric trains which run every 10 minutes.

Just before Easter my good ear went on strike for a time and left me completely stone deaf, so I was sent to Downside to make my retreat (!) and to be under the doctor there, who eventually got it right again with penicillin. On my way back I was able to go to the funeral in London of my nice Irish Guards general whom I went to after I left you in Limerick. Though it was very sad to lose him, it was lovely to be able to go to the service in the Guards Chapel, as he had always been so kind about coming to see me here—he came over specially for the day just after Christmas. And I found that the Irish Guards were on duty at Buckingham Palace, so they invited me to lunch and collected all the men who had been with me in the war.

We now have a midday Mass here every day, as the rules for fasting have been relaxed, and it is wonderful to see the hundreds and hundreds who come pouring in every day—we have to have two priests giving Holy Communion and another one hearing Confessions. But unless Downside sends another priest—which seems like wishing for the moon—it means that we are all completely tied every day of the year from 12 till 2. You _must_ come and see them when you are here, as they are such good people, and you get lovely contrasts—old Irish women in shawls kneeling next to shipping or cotton magnates.

I can still hardly believe that you will perhaps be here in a month's time!

You _are_ angelic to suggest it.

With my fondest love to you both—
Julian

St Mary's
Highfield St.
Liverpool, 3

Dearest Noreen,

Have booked you a room, with bathroom, at the Blundellsands Hotel (Tel. Great Crosby 3883) from Thursday, June 20th to Saturday June 22nd—which would give us all Friday, which is my least busy day that week. Thursday is Corpus Christi, but it is only in the morning and afternoon that I will be busy.

I almost feel inclined to advise you not to come up by car—as it is a terrible drive—built up all the way—and the good trains are very good. "The Red Rose" leaves Euston at 12.30 and is in Liverpool by 4—(it is absolutely non-stop) and ten minutes later there is an electric train right to the back door of your hotel. And on Saturday (when I will have Confessions all the evening) there is a 3 o'clock back which gets to London just after 7, or, if you had to go earlier, "the Merseyside Express" leaves Liverpool at 10.10 and is in London (non-stop) at 1.45.

Bless you both a <u>thousand</u> times for coming.

With all my love—
Julian

St Mary's Priory
Highfield Street
Liverpool, 3

Sunday

Dearest Noreen,

As I am writing this, the weather couldn't be more perfect, so I am hoping you will have a lovely crossing tomorrow, and, of course, I will be thinking of you all the time. We have a real heat-wave here waiting for you.

I have managed to keep all Friday free except for giving Communion at the 12.30 Mass and hearing confessions for an hour afterwards (1–2), but Saturday has proved almost impossible to keep free from 11 o'clock onwards, so I feel I ought to let you go on the morning train, which would give you more time to see people at the weekend. The Merseyside Express leaves here at 10.10. and is non-stop to London, where it arrives at 1.45.

Incidentally, I have a cottage for you to buy on Tuesday the 24th!! It is even more of a dream than the one on Galway Bay. It is at Lulworth, and has the most unbelievably lovely view all along the wildest part of the Dorset coast (I will show you a photograph when you come) and, of course, is much more civilized than the one in Ireland, as it has electric light, running water, a bathroom, and a garage.

About your coming here—in case you can't get me on the telephone, I will meet the Red Rose at 4 o'clock, (in case you are on it) and suggest that you go straight to your hotel, which is only a few yards from the sea, and have a cool tea out in the garden after the train journey, and I will join you there after the evening Mass (at which we try and fit 1,000 people into a church made for 400), which lasts from 5.30 to just after 6, and then I hope to be able to stay with you for the rest of the evening.

Your hotel is almost the last house on the outskirts of Liverpool, so we will be able to escape into the country quite easily—either into the country part of Lancashire (there is a complete Catholic village call Little Crosly only a mile away and Ince Blundell Hall where your and my nearest ancestress in common, Catherine Blundell, came from, is only two miles away).

I don't know how I will get through the next 96 hours! Bless
you both a <u>thousand</u> times for your kindness in coming.

With fondest love—
Julian

In case you arrive at any other time when I can't meet you—from
Lime Street station where you arrive it is only two minutes in a
taxi to the Exchange Station (beside our church), and from there
there are electric trains every ten minutes from the platform on
the left to "Blundellsands & Crosly", and when you get out there
the hotel is literally the other side of the road.

St Mary's
Liverpool, 3
1 Sept. 1957

Dearest Noreen,

It was so lovely getting yours and Pam's sweet letters on my birthday. Now that you have been here twice, and with the boats going and coming from America every day, you seem <u>far</u> closer here than anywhere else I have ever been.

I will be seeing all the cousins on Wednesday night. Edith Sitwell is giving a Poetry Reading at the Dorchester in aid of the Chapel Fund, and I can just fit it in on my journey, and on the way back I have promised to spend one night at Stonor, if I possibly can, to see your father, as it was such a great disappointment having to be away just when he was coming specially to Liverpool. I had such a nice letter from him, saying that he had very good news for me, so, of course, I didn't tell him that you had already let me into the secret.

It was so nice of you to remember the poor little blind mother. She has come back from Lourdes with her eye so much better that the doctors are not going to remove it for the present, as they now think that they may be able to restore the sight.

I will send you some official accounts of the Exhibition, which starts on the 30th. One of the nicest parts has been the tremendous interest and kindness of the new Archbishop. I have spent many hours with him and his great charm and kindness has done so much to make up for the coldness of the Abbot.

Molly's address is Mrs. Barrett, St Katherine's House, Savernake Forest, Marlborough, Wilts—St Katherine's being the unused church at the end of her garden, as her house used to be the Vicarage.

Your other question in a previous letter, which I have a feeling I never answered was about the article on those ferocious fair-haired Celts in "Life", which you read on the plane. You will be glad to hear that they were <u>not</u> our forefathers. About 20 years ago some professors changed the word 'Celt' which for centuries had referred to the dark Mediterranean peoples, whom they now call 'Iberians', to mean the later invaders from North

Germany and Russia, but 99 people out of 100 still use 'Celtic' for the dark people.

I hope you will be able to read this small writing, but I want to enclose a note to Pam and am afraid three pages would be too heavy to go by air. With fondest love and blessings to you all four—

from Julian

St. Mary's Priory,
Highfield Street,
Liverpool, 3.
22.10.57

My dearest Noreen,

I am afraid I couldn't write to Johnny for the 6th, as I was in the throes of a violent attack of Asian 'flu, so this letter will bring you <u>both</u> all my love and blessings for your new year together...

Apart from your wonderful visit in June, the great joy of this last year was, of course, seeing your father again and seeing him look so <u>marvellously</u> well and happy, and knowing how much you two had to do with it. And it was so lovely to hear from Sherman last week, saying what a "most happy visit" it had been and how much they had all loved having him...

I was down with 'flu during all but the first two days of the Exhibition, but considering that its fortnight coincided with the worst of the epidemic, I think it was well worth all the work. It was visited by 40,000 in the fortnight, and the record for Liverpool was the 41,000 who visited the Van Gogh exhibition, which went on for <u>five</u> weeks. I have had wonderfully kind messages about it from everyone, and, financially, it made over £1,000 for the new Cathedral.

The first edition of the book (a paper-covered one) came out before the Exhibition was over and sold 800 copies. I will send you one as a tiny birthday present; as you will remember Ince Blundell and Paddington; and next time you come I must show you the really lovely coloured film we have made—which runs for about three quarters of an hour.

With my fondest love and a million blessings to you both, and of course my thoughts will be with.... [last line of original photocopy letter missing]

Julian

Downside Abbey
Stratton on the Fosse, Bath
15 April 1958

Dearest Noreen,

I have just arrived here for three days of retreat and so am seizing the chance of answering your lovely but very sad letter of a few weeks ago. I had hoped so much to get a letter off to Nicky for his birthday yesterday, but I never even finished the most urgent official letters and forms and have had to bring a great bundle of them here to do in my retreat. I do hope he was home with you for his birthday, in which case he won't have missed a letter.

But, to return to your letter, although all the details were so sad—poor little Georgie being told to ask for money instead of that lovely dress, and Sherman selling all the farmlands to meet their extravagant bills—it has left me in a great glow of happiness, which I can see is never going to fade, because of the unbelievably wonderful news that, if it was put up for sale, your darling Johnny would buy it. The thought of you living there as your home conjures up such thrilling pictures that I just can't let myself think about it too much, as I find myself longing to hear that it is for sale! You would all four fit in to it so perfectly, and at last the peace and happiness of the people would match the lovely setting. And, of course, the village would be absolutely thrilled with joy. It really would be heaven on earth.

I am hoping to get a fortnight's holiday at the end of July and, if so, am going to try out a rehearsal for when you come over next year. I have found a man in the west of Ireland who hires out lovely horse-drawn caravans—complete with little sleeping cabins, gas fires and light, linen, crockery, etc., all for £3 or £4 a week. Can you imagine anything more peaceful than plodding along those lovely Connemara lanes behind a horse and camping on the edge of the sea?

With my fondest love to you all—

Julian

Cumberland
1 Sept. 1958

Dearest Noreen,

At last I have managed to get away for the first time this year, as an Indian priest came to stay for a week. So I have come to a farm up here (nowhere near Egremont, alas!) where I can be completely undisturbed and can concentrate on answering a whole year's accumulation of letters.

It sounds so hard for you too to know how to act—certainly in the tragic affair about the house, which really does look like the end of it. One thing that has consoled me more than anything now that the end seems almost inevitable is the remembrance of how many even of our own ancestors have given up even lovelier heritages than Stonor because they saw how absolutely momentary and almost meaningless was anything in this world compared with eternity. One thing which I always mean to show you when you come over, and always forget, is a table I once made out of all the canonized Saints and Martyrs I am descended from—about two thirds of them are through my mother, but most of them you will share as they are usually through a large number of different descents: of direct descents from a married saint or martyr I have traced nearly five thousand; from the brother or sister of one who was a priest or a nun over eight thousand; and more than twenty-four thousand altogether, counting descents from uncles or aunts. And when one thinks that every normal lifetime spans five generations, because we normally know our grand-parents and our grandchildren, and that only three such lifetimes take us back to Saint Thomas More, for instance, from whom we are both descended, it makes them seem amazingly close.

But it is the knowledge of what they all gave up so cheerfully that I find such a strength in the face of the giving-up of Stonor, or, in my case, the having to give up all the things I love most in the world—the world of birds and flowers and animals and mountains; because all the many martyrs among them gave up life itself and the others were mostly queens and princesses, who gave up lovely homes and everything they could want in order to become nuns in very strict orders like the Poor Clares.

I will give you the names of some of them because I am sure darling Pam and Nicky would like to know at school that people who might seem rather unreal as figures in history books were every bit as truly their ancestors as you and Johnny.

Among our absolutely direct ancestors are Saint Louis IX, King of France (925 times in my case); Saint Margaret, Queen of Scotland (over 600 times); Saint Ealhswitha, the wife of King Alfred the Great (over a thousand times); Saint Ferdinand III, King of Castile; Saint Elizabeth, Queen of Portugal; and, of course, martyrs like Saint Thomas More; Blessed Margaret Pole, the niece of King Edward IV who lived at Bockmer; and Blessed Adrian Fortescue who lived at Stonor, and after it being his home for 34 years had it taken away from him!

I am still hoping to try the Irish gypsy-caravans, if only for a week; but these three days have been the first I have been able to get away from Liverpool. It really would be heaven if you four could come and do it next year—along the Kerry coast where there are miles and miles of sandy beaches without a soul on them, and lovely beehive cells built by the Irish monks of Saint Patrick's time on the cliffs among the clumps of sea-pinks and the sea-gulls; and we could live on fresh mackerel which we could catch ourselves, eggs, home-made bread, and butter, cheese and cream galore!

With all my love to each of you—Julian

18.10.58

Highfield Street

Liverpool 3

Dearest Noreen,

I actually started a letter to Johnny for October 6th, but was never able to finish it; and now, even if I manage to finish this letter by tonight I am beginning to fear that you may not get it on the 26th, and I am not at all sure where to send it to—whether you will still be up in Newport (I imagine your mother will long to keep you there for your birthday) or will have already gone down to Florida—where I am not at all sure of your right address. But at any rate you will know that I will be thinking of you all the time whether you hear from me or not.

I haven't heard any more news from Stonor, as none of the family there ever write, except very occasionally Sherman—about once a year. And it is so long since I have seen it, or any of them, that I almost feel as if it had gone already. The last time must have been after my illness in Cumberland more than four years ago.

If it wasn't for my occasional glimpses of all the love and happiness which radiate from you four, I feel I wouldn't really have any ties left on earth, because, fond as I am of my sister, Molly, she is a completely independent and self-sufficient character, luckily, and she wrote the other day that she is as happy as can be in her new little thatch-roofed cottage: The Castle Cottage, Lockeridge, Marlborough, Wilts.

My own life seems to have reached a complete dead-end. Even if I live to be 70—only another 20 years—there doesn't seem to be any hope of my spending any more of it at Downside. I have only been allowed to spend three years there, when my mother begged for it after my illness at Worth after the war, in the 28 years since I left the novitiate. And my last chance of being given one of our five country parishes, because three have already been given to people much younger than me and the other two given to people even younger. So I am afraid it is a life-sentence for me in this grim city.

And there is sad news from my beloved Peasedown and Wellow. Both the chapels have now been sold. At Wellow there won't be

131

any more services at all, while at Peasedown there will only be a priest coming out from Bath on Sunday mornings to say Mass in the local cinema.

I am so sorry this has been such a sad letter for your birthday, but you and Johnny are the only people I can turn to for sympathy—and you both give it so generously and understandingly that it is terribly hard not to take advantage of you.

Bless you all four—and with lots and lots of love to <u>you</u> on the 26th—

Yours always—
Julian

13 May 1959

St. Mary's Priory
Highfield Street
Liverpool, 3

My dearest Noreen,

My nice namesake from Portsmouth Priory was so thrilled and surprised to meet you in Virginia and, like everyone else, was enraptured by what a lovely person Pam has become and how like you. He wrote to me the very same day to tell me what a joy it had been to him to meet you again.

Last night I was asked by the Anglican Dean here to give a talk to his clergy and congregation on "Why I am a Roman Catholic". They simply couldn't have been nicer and kinder and the meeting lasted three hours! The Dean turned out to be a cousin of Nadine's husband. He is a Father Christopher Pepys. He was a naval chaplain in the war, and so nice. I am asking Sherman to invite him over to Stonor, as he often stays at Oxford.

I expect you have heard the lovely job Thomas has been given for the five months until he is due to go up to Oxford—as tutor to the Crown Prince of Nepal in Katmandu, with all his expenses paid and £300 pocket money. The only sad thing must be the feeling that it will almost inevitably be the next victim of the Chinese communists after Tibet.

Apparently Francis went out with him, and Archbishop Mathew, who came to visit me recently, said that Francis often stays at Stonor now and that relations seem to be very friendly. I don't know what the official position is.

I am afraid my own position seems as gloomy as ever and no chance of even a few days' retreat or holiday this year.

A short time ago the Abbot offered me the chaplaincy to an old ladies' home in the Cotswolds—but he cancelled it a few weeks later, and said that I was to remain on as a curate here. The most humiliating part—which has given rise to all sorts of rumours among the Liverpool clergy—is that though I am now the senior curate (the other one having left at Easter) and am 50 years old and have been a priest for a quarter of a century, whenever the parish priest goes away he sends up a young monk from Downside "to take charge"—so far, ones who have never even spent a day on a parish in their lives.

I know it ought to be very good for me, but I am afraid it isn't.

With all my love to you both—and hoping that Pam will prove a worthy daughter of her father and sweep off all the prizes at Foxcroft next month—

Always your affectionate
Julian

9 August 1959

Dearest Noreen,

It seems quite incredible what they were able to do to your poor Nicky, and all in one operation. He must have been under the anesthetic for hours, and the strain on you and Johnny and Pam must have been simply terrible. Thank goodness you are all back in Newport together now, and Nicky is able to breath nothing but strong sea air. And I am sure that by Pam's great day on the 15th he will be feeling well enough to really enjoy it. That Saturday, the patronal feast of our church here (our Lady's Assumption), will be a terribly busy day, but I will, of course, be thinking of you all all day and wishing special blessings on darling Pam, that she may always be as lovely in character as she is in bodily beauty. And, luckily, it is one of the days on which we are each allowed to offer two Masses, the second one for any intention we like, and so <u>my</u> second one, of course, will be for Pam's intentions—including, I know, deep gratitude to God for Nicky's recovery.

If you do take a house around Biarritz next summer, you will only be a mile or two from where my father is buried at St Jean de Luz, so if I do manage to come and see you there (though I am afraid it is very, very unlikely) I would be able to visit his grave, which I have never seen. And I would love to go to Lourdes with you all.

But this year it was only at the very last minute that I was able to get away for a week, when a young monk from Downside came here for a week very unexpectedly. It was mostly a very rushed round of visits in the south, but it included one heavenly day at the White City (which I first visited with <u>you</u>), to see Jane Kent about her wedding in March, which she wants me to do. Her mother asked so much about you, and a nice Mrs Robinson (her husband, who used to judge horses, had just died), who wants to call and see you in New York in the fall, and, of course, the Haydons (Cynthia won everything that day, including the supreme championship for the fourth year running). She too has had a sad summer as her elder son, Richard, who was much closer to her than the younger one, was killed at Oxford.

With my fondest love to you all four—and may the 15th be an absolutely unforgettable day for you all. I will go down and dip my hand into <u>your</u> Atlantic to feel a bit nearer!

Your affectionate
Julian

Liverpool
4 Sept 1959

Dearest Noreen,

It was so lovely to get your and Pam's letters on my birthday morning. It hasn't really sunken in yet that I am now an old man of fifty, but at least it means that I can't have more than about twenty years here—and looking back to twenty years ago today (the day I was called up as a chaplain) the time has flown past, and so I hope the remaining twenty will go just as quick.

It was wonderful to hear from you both how perfect Pam's party was and that dear Nicky was able to take part in it. As you know, I always think that you four have kept that original happiness and goodness of the first family in Paradise. Usually one only sees it in the eyes of babies and very small children under seven, before sin has come in to spoil them and make them self-conscious, and in the affection which the higher animals, like horses and dogs, give, if we love them. One realizes then what the world would have been like, if sin had never entered into it. I am sure it is because of his goodness—physical, mental and spiritual—that Nicky has made such a wonderfully quick recovery—and I love the thought of Johnny and Pam spending hours sailing in the sunshine. I am sure the physical good which the sea and the sun must do them is matched by the goodness which subconsciously seeps into their minds and souls in a world so clean and good that the very thought of sin and evil becomes impossible with the sea all round you and sun and the breeze reminding you all the time of God's goodness.

One thing I meant to ask you last time I wrote: Can you sponsor people you have never seen for getting a visa to America? There are two charming Catholic girls here—Marie Keight (pronounced KEET) and Patricia Waterman—aged about 28, who have set their hearts on going to America for at least a year, when the fare by air comes down to £64 after October 15. They have each spent ten years as the person to whom you make "enquiries" at the two main-line stations here—a maddening job, I would have thought, but they seem to possess absolutely inexhaustible charm and kindness and patience and the Railway will miss them terribly. They are hoping to get jobs in America that will enable them to travel to the south and west as well as the east coast—if possible, together—and are willing to sign on for more than a year if necessary. If you can think of anything for them—secretary, companion, children's nurse, etc—do let me know, as Marie, whom I know best, is a really quite exceptionally charming and good person, and as well as being very pretty they are both extremely efficient and hard-working. "British Railways" would give them a wonderful character.

With my fondest love to you all—

Julian

21 Oct. 1959

My dearest Noreen—

I forget whether I told you that two of the three new priests here came from the States, though British by birth. One spent four or five years as a parish priest in California and the other has just come back from a long holiday in Newark. The result is that they take a number of American papers, and it was lovely yesterday to see a coloured photograph of your beautiful Pam, looking lovelier than ever in a silver wig, at a party at The Breakers, and a smaller one of you talking to John Brown.

Although it was probably several weeks ago, I am presuming from it that you are still at Newport—I expect your mother insists on having you near for your birthday!—so I will send my love and good wishes to you there, and hope my letter will arrive in time.

My own affairs have reached what I hope is their final crisis, after 28 years of fruitless appeals to be allowed a certain amount of peace and quiet. What finally brought things to a head was a deception of the Abbot's so cynical and typical of all his few dealings with me that I suddenly realized that he hadn't the least intention of <u>ever</u> making things easier for me. As you know, he has stopped my holidays and even the three days of the annual eight-day retreat at Downside which one of us used to be able to get, and the pressure of work here has been increased even more, so that I just couldn't face it for the rest of my life. So I drew up a long appeal to Rome, giving the whole story of his treatment of me, and begging to be allowed to retire into private life as a layman. When I sent a copy to the Abbot about 6 months ago, he wouldn't read it, but he did write suggesting that he get me a chaplaincy to a Benedictine convent. When I asked him if he really meant it or if it was just a passing kind thought, he assured me that he did, but that there was no convent vacant just then. A week or two ago, a lovely Benedictine convent on the South Devon coast (one of which several of our ancestors had been Abbesses) wrote to him for a chaplain. Immediately, without a word to me, he offered them a young monk who has never had to leave Downside since he joined. When I protested, he merely wrote back that he hoped I would be happier at Liverpool under the new régime.

So both Molly and Sherman separately offered to go and remon-
strate with the Abbot over his continued ill-treatment of me,
and, if they have no effect, I have decided that the only thing is
for me to put my case to Rome and ask to be dispensed from a
life which is so utterly different from the one to which I vowed
myself and which becomes so much more unbearable when one
feels nothing but bitterness and hatred towards the person whom
one is meant to look upon as Our Lord Himself.

They have both asked for appointments with him in the next
few days, so perhaps by your birthday I will know my fate. My
idea is to retire to somewhere very quiet in Ireland, and try to
get a job on a farm with horses or animals, and hope that I will
gradually forget the Abbot's deceptions and humiliations so that I
will be able to bring myself to forgive him in my heart before I die.

With all my love and blessings—to you all

Your affectionate

Julian

Liverpool
16.11.59

Dearest Noreen,

Thank you so much for telling me the terribly sad news about your father. I am, of course, putting him first in my prayers all the time, and I do hope it will prove to be one of those completely painless cases that I have witnessed in the hospital here again and again. It is the death I would most like to die myself, because one's brain remains completely clear almost to the very end. And death is such a lovely thing really, <u>far</u> the most wonderfully happy moment of one's whole life.

All our blindness and misunderstanding and fear suddenly vanishes for ever, and we really see for the first time how much Our Lord has loved us all the time. He Himself was so bubbling over with joy and happiness once He had come back from the grave and conquered death for us all that he spent most of his time deliberately teasing us. "<u>Why</u> are you crying? <u>Who</u> are you looking for?", he asked Mary Magdalen, pretending He was a gardener. "<u>Why</u> are you so sad as you walk along? <u>What</u> has happened?", he asked the disciples on the road to Emmaus, and <u>pretended</u> He was going farther until they pressed Him to stay with them and tell them more. And how can one be frightened when one remembers that it is the same Son of God who will be there to meet us who got up early in the morning while it was still dark, took a bag of charcoal down to the shore of the lake, and when he saw a fishing boat passing by in the dim light about a quarter of a mile out, called out, "Children, have you got anything to eat with your bread?"—(and again He <u>knew</u> they hadn't, but it was more tactful than to ask them if they had caught any fish!)—and then, after giving them the breakfast he had cooked on the beach, still teasing them by not telling them who He was, He took Saint Peter for a walk along the beach and made him—quite unconsciously—cancel out his three denials by his three outbursts of "But, Lord, you <u>know</u> that I love Thee". As you can see, we just <u>can't</u> be afraid of meeting someone like that, especially as He Himself has told us that the first thing He will do will be to wipe away all tears from our eyes, if there are any there.

It was sweet of you to send me the little booklet about St Gregory's Priory in Michigan. Actually I think you had got them confused with Fr Gregory's ones at Elmira in New York State—he is a great friend of mine and Father Julian Stead's—the ones in Michigan are very High Church Anglicans, but I was most moved and interested by what they were doing, but my fate is already sealed. I am not meant to know, but a friend at Downside has warned me that, unknown to me, I am to be seen by a Jewish psychiatrist employed for the school at Downside, who is to recommend that I be given so much to do that I won't have time to hanker after silence and prayer. It is incredible that the Abbot can still believe that after trying it for over thirty years!

I am very worried about my two charming girls—they are absolutely charming in every way—as they have now booked their passage on the Carinthia, sailing from here on Nov. 27th and reaching New York about Dec. 6th, but I expect they will be allright and in any case you obviously mustn't worry about anything else now—

With my fondest love—and bless you more than ever now for what you did for your father spiritually a year or two ago—

Your loving

Julian

25.3.60

Dearest Noreen,

Suddenly, with the spring, everything seems to be taking a turn for the better.

First and foremost, I am thrilled to hear from Sherman that you are so much better that you have been able to go to Florida and that Johnny and Pam have been able to leave you, which I know they would never have done if there had been even the slightest danger.

Then, tomorrow, I go to Stonor for a week, to help prepare for the reopening of the Chapel by the Archbishop on the evening of Sunday, April 3rd—a reopening which, of course, you have done more than everyone else combined to make possible; so that all my prayers that evening will be for you.

And, finally, although my future is still far from certain and I don't see any prospect for a long time yet of being able to unpack all my things, which I had to pack so suddenly on the night of January 2nd, I do think that things are beginning to move towards a happier future.

A week or so ago the Abbot wrote and apologized for all the suffering that his "faults and inadequacies" had caused me during the last fourteen years, and is talking of sending me in July to be chaplain to a convent of Benedictine nuns in North Wales, where I am going on April 4th for a fortnight to help them through Holy Week and Easter. So at last I see a hope of some peace and quiet, though, after so many previous disappointments, I won't really believe it until it actually happens.

But at least during these next three weeks, at Stonor and Talacre, you know that my thoughts will be often and often with you, and thanking God from the depth of my heart for sparing you to us.

With all my love—
Julian

5 April 1960

Dearest Noreen,

I am writing this letter from Talacre Abbey in North Wales, where I arrived last night for a fortnight and, of course, I am longing to tell you about my heavenly week at Stonor and its wonderful climax on Sunday evening, which, even though you weren't there, was still the happiest hour in the whole of my fifty years, because you were so close in spirit all the time. In fact, for the whole week you were hardly ever out of my thoughts except for odd moments.

I am <u>longing</u> for you to see what you have enabled Sherman to do for the Chapel, because it really is absolutely a dream of beauty (John Piper chose the colour-scheme after years of thought) and the very best stone-mason in England (an old Irish Guardsman of mine) did the re-construction.

The re-dedication ceremony was so lovely that, although the chapel and the tribune were absolutely packed, you could have heard a pin drop at any moment of the service. The Archbishop, who has a lovely soft musical voice, said a low Mass at six in the evening (the chapel was lit by candle-light and the sunset glow on the walls, which in any case are now a lovely rose colour, with a blue ceiling), and there was no other sound except a tremendous chorus of birds singing outside. He preached a most moving sermon.

Bobby, who is still as good-looking as ever, but has improved out of all recognition in character, served the Archbishop, and Jeanne and her three daughters, in black with mantillas, looked so lovely when they went up to Communion that one had to hold one's breath—and I know it was a real holiness, and not just appearances, because they had all been to confession just before and were as moved by the whole thing as Sherman and I were.

Georgie, of course, has the strongest character, but it is difficult to say which is the more lovely in appearance between Julia and Harriet—Julia, though 21 on the 19th, is just innocence personified and one just can't imagine her ever doing anything wrong, whereas Harriet is more sophisticated and, since her illness, has become even more shy and elusive than before.

They all three work tremendously hard—Julia is now the head of the religious department of Asprey's in Bond Street, and Georgina and Harriet, besides doing a tremendous amount in the house and kitchen, are studying about six subjects at Reading Technical College from 9 till 5 every day.

Sherman was, of course an absolutely perfect host afterwards. About 100 people came in for drinks and about 30 stayed for dinner—a dinner cooked entirely by Jeanne and Harriet.

Ruby Heath had been very ill, but luckily began to get better the day I arrived, and got up for the first time the day I left. Two dear old faithful workmen had died since I was there last, Mr. West and Mr. Combes, and George Sherfield had just had a very serious operation. So I went down to the village almost every day, and, of course, they all loved talking about you. Georgie and Bobby are very good about visiting them regularly.

One other nice thing that happened while I was there was a pure white doe which suddenly appeared among the deer.

The news of Francis is fairly good though he is still in hospital.

With my fondest love, Noreen, and I am not sure whether Nicky is with you or with the others—but if he is with you, please give him my special love and blessing on the 16th.

Always yours affectionate
Julian

Talacre Abbey

Gronant

Prestatyn

North Wales

24 August 1960

Dearest Noreen,

It is so lovely to be able to write to you again at last. For months nobody seemed to know where you were except vaguely "going to Switzerland" or "in Switzerland". But even in my wildest dreams I never dreamt such a <u>wonderful</u> surprise as you have given me. Little does the baby know what a <u>heavenly</u> life is in store for it in the one absolutely perfect family in the world. And I think it is such a lovely time for you and Johnny, because just when you will have to steel yourselves to parting with darling Pam and Nicky you will have this new child in its most absorbing and loveable years.

It was so sweet of you to go and see my mother's grave in that lovely lakeside cemetery. I am sure she prayed very hard for you both that day, because she knows how much I love you both.

I would give anything to be at Shannon and see your plane circling down again, but, though I will start scheming I don't see very much hope. I absolutely <u>love</u> it here, with my own little house on the mountainside, but I am very <u>tied</u> as the nuns have to have a priest for the various services and it is very hard to find a substitute. But you know I will be there in spirit all through your flight.

With my very fondest love and blessings to you all—and heartfelt congratulations—

from Julian

Talacre Abbey
Gronant
Prestatyn
North Wales
26.9.60

My dearest Noreen,

Sherman came up to see me last week and told me that he was very worried about you, without being able to say why. (He also gave me my first news of darling Pam's motor-bicycle accident, so that I now have a <u>double</u> worry). I do hope that you are all right and that the long plane flight and the anxiety about Pam haven't taken too much out of you after your own terribly long illness and now the additional strain—heavenly though it is—of the new baby, and I suppose the hundreds and hundreds of friends who will be coming to congratulate you day after day.

I hope you got my note at Shannon Airport, as they didn't return it to me, and that you perhaps had time to see some of the little white cabins and the Irish donkeys.

I don't want to add even one letter to your correspondence at a time when you must try to conserve all your strength, and in any case I will, of course, be writing again for your birthday in a few weeks; but so that I can get some really first-hand news of you, I am asking a great friend of mine in New York to see if you are there, but, if you are in Newport, could you please get either Johnny or one of the children to send a line to reassure me.

The friend in New York is a sweet Sister from the Eye Hospital which I used to visit in Liverpool, who is now doing a year in the Manhattan Eye Hospital. Her name is Margaret Ambrose, she adores all animals, rides beautifully, has a lovely Boxer (back at home) and now has to console herself with the squirrels in Central Park. She was very lucky coming over in the Parthia, because she found a lovely black hunter stallion on board being taken to a stud in America and, being wonderful with horses, more or less took charge of it.

I do a certain amount of riding here in this heavenly hill country by the sea. The Welsh countryside is not <u>quite</u> as lovely as the Cumberland Fells and lakes, but it is very similar and I absolutely love it. But next month I have to decide whether to leave my peace and independence here and go to look after the coach parties and pilgrimages at Stonor. There is no need to tell <u>you</u> what things I love there and what things I dread, but do pray that I make the right decision after my retreat at Downside from October 12th to 20th, as the Abbot is leaving the decision to me.

With my fondest love and blessings to you all four—and to your dear father when you next see him—and <u>please</u> take the greatest care of yourself.

Julian

Downside
19.10.60

Dearest Noreen,

I am leaving here in a few minutes, but will be travelling about for two or three days, so I <u>must</u> write now to make sure it reaches you in time to bring you all my love on the 26th and my deepest, deepest, congratulations on the wonderful news about next February. Dear little Harriet, whom I saw at the funeral of the Reverend Mother at Ascot last week, told me the date.

Why I have left it to the last minutes of my stay here to write to you is because the Abbot wouldn't make up his mind about my future until the end of my retreat, and I have only just come from him a few moments ago.

He has agreed, what I have felt more and more clearly inside, that I ought to stay where I am at Talacre—with the peace and regularity of the monastic life and the lovely sung Mass and Offices every day, and that all the attractions to Stonor are purely <u>human</u> ones, which one is meant to sacrifice when one leaves everything to follow Our Lord—my affections for Sherman and all the family, for the people round about in the village and like the Pipers, and my love of the place itself and the Chiltern countryside.

I am afraid dear Sherman will be bitterly disappointed, and I do <u>hate</u> having to hurt him. Because I really do think he is happier when I am there, and we share all the same tastes and hobbies.

I <u>do</u> hope you are really well and I am sure your doctor and Johnny and your mother all combined will <u>insist</u> that you have a quieter and more restful Fall and Winter than you can usually manage to get. I can't help hoping myself that you will stay in Newport and not go back to New York till it is all over.

Incidentally, Harriet told me the wonderful news of how much better your father is, and that he is even driving a car again and talking of a visit to England.

With my fondest love to you all, and a very, <u>very</u>, Happy Birthday.   from
                                                                Julian

149

Talacre
25 Nov. 1960

Dearest Noreen,

Thank you <u>so</u> much for being so kind to Margaret Ambrose. She wrote, the next day, to say that it was far the loveliest evening she had had in America, and she thought you were looking awfully well with no sign of having been so ill. She too gave me the most glowing description of your little baby and your games of hide-and-seek with her. She hadn't given me a hint that she was finding the nursing and the living conditions harder than in England. I had always imagined that they were <u>miles</u> better.

Of course, I am praying all the time about February 14th. A lovely girl from Liverpool, whose wedding I did shortly before I left, came out to see me last weekend, and she seemed so well that I took her up a mountain to see a prehistoric fort that is being excavated, and, two days later!, she has had the most lovely son born.

I am afraid I am back in the blackest of black books at Stonor. About a month ago I had a very painful letter from Sherman, reproaching me with my "change of heart", and though I have written him two long letters since to try to explain my point of view I haven't heard a word. Perhaps it shows that, as you said, I would only have got hurt again if I <u>had</u> gone, as they both get such difficult moods when things go wrong.

I do hope you were both pleased with the result of the Presidential election. From what one could read over here, he seemed so much nicer of the two men—a real idealist and not only a professional politician. But the difference between the two parties is always beyond me!

I hear your father is holding his own most <u>wonderfully</u>. Do give him my love and tell him how pleased I am—and, of course, my deepest love to all five of you—

Bless you always—
Julian

150

Talacre
27 Nov. 1960

Dearest Noreen,

I remembered too late that in my last letter I had never answered your query about the sins of parents being visited on their children. <u>You</u> certainly needn't worry, but what it means is that, owing to the whole nature of parenthood and heredity, the characters of the parents, whether good or evil, do come out in children, even to the third, fourth, or seventh generation, as we often see in practice. But the whole of the Old and New Testament are <u>full</u> of passages telling us that this doesn't affect our free will or personal responsibility. The Prophet Ezekiel, for example, was furious with the Jews for repeating the proverb: "The fathers ate sour grapes and the children's teeth were set on edge"—(Chapter 18).

What reminded me of it was a lovely example of heredity I have seen on the television in the lodge-keeper's cottage. It was the clothing of a nun for the Little Company of Mary—a nursing order who look after the dying, by prayer and by actual nursing. Only the happiest people come through the probationary period and this girl of 21 had the most beautiful and happy face I have ever seen. She came in dressed as a bride—the title of the program was "Love is my Vocation"—and her smile to the priest, who was questioning her, and to her dear old mother when she passed her as she came in and went out of the chapel were absolutely breath-taking in the way they lit up her face and several of the hard-bitten reviewers in the papers who saw it last week (it was re-layed a week late to Wales) admitted that they found tears streaming down their cheeks. But the point is that she was a wonderful example of heredity, because she came from that lovely Catholic island in the Outer Hebrides—South Uist—(now, alas, being made into a rockets base) and only generations of goodness could have given her that heavenly happiness and goodness and that transparently <u>spiritual</u> beauty, which was yet so natural—her father was killed in the war, but the mother, who was giving her only child to God, looked just as lovely as the daughter—who, she said, had always loved dancing and singing—and indeed she had a lovely Hebridean voice, but had always wanted to be a nursing nun.

Another good example is Donna Fabriola, who is marrying the Belgian King—though so beautiful and so rich, she has always been to Mass and Communion at 6 since she was a small child and has spent almost all her time looking after the poorest of the poor or the very sick. All her family took it for granted that she would be a nun too. Instead, she will transmit that loveliness of character to her children, and, if they are faithful, to her children's children. Just as you and Johnny will do—

Bless you always—

Julian

Talacre Abbey
Gronant
15.12.60

My dearest Noreen,

As you can imagine, I have hardly been able to think of anything else since getting your letter. And, of course, your name always comes first at every Mass I offer and in every prayer.

I <u>do</u> hope that no more news in the last few days means good news—and that there is no longer any real risk of the child being born too soon. I went into Liverpool last weekend to baptize such a <u>lovely</u> baby, but I am sure yours will be far lovelier.

Even apart from the baby, thank goodness you are being kept in bed. Because the descriptions even in the English papers of your blizzards in New York make me shiver even in the lovely warm Welsh sunshine, with all the birds singing.

I have had nice greetings from all the Stonor children, including a telephone message from Thomas, just off to Austria the next morning. (I didn't of course tell them your news). But not a word from Sherman and Jeanne yet, though I will try and find them an extra nice Christmas card—as I do <u>hate</u> hurting poor Sherman.

Did I tell you that that sweet Mother Perpetua whom you once met at Ascot, is now the head of the whole order in England! She is so fond of you and always asks about you in every letter.

May the next two months pass very, very quickly for you, and leave you at the end of them the happiest person in the whole world. And then we really must start planning how <u>we</u> are going to meet again. It seems such a long, long time ago since I saw you in Liverpool. Ince Blundell is now a convent.

With all my fondest love to you—and to you all—
and a <u>big</u> blessing—
from
Julian

Talacre Abbey
16.7.61

Dearest Noreen,

Of all your many letters during the last fourteen years, your last was far and away the loveliest and I read it again and again.

It's so wonderful that you have been able to nurse your adorable Pussy Willow yourself after your long illness and be so well. I <u>love</u> that heavenly coloured photograph of you, which I have in front of me whenever I am indoors—and you look so fantastically young to be a mother at all, least of all to have a grown-up daughter and a son of six foot five.

Everybody who met her says the same lovely things about Pam as you write, and she completely bowled over the family at Stonor by her loveliness and the tremendous charm of her personality. Jeanne was as overwhelmed as anyone and kept saying how she wished I could <u>see</u> her when she rang up to tell me that I would be hearing Pam's voice on the telephone.

Darling Julia is, of course, the one I now envy, seeing so much of you all. And she does realize how lucky she is, and she is, of course, enormously impressed by Nicky.

I am sure you were wise to sell your big house in Newport, though I wish you had somewhere to which you could escape from all the hundreds of people who must be wanting to see you all the time—though I do sympathize with them, as it must do them so much good to be in the presence of the one <u>perfectly</u> happy family in the world.

I hope I can remember the wording of the two poems, I think one was:

> My son, the God of Heaven has a son,
> No bigger than thou art; and, silently,
> <u>His</u> mother rocks his cot, when day is done,
> And watches <u>him</u>, even as I watch thee.
>
> Sleep, little one (that shall not wake again);
> Across the way the Prince of Peace is born,
> Who brings <u>us</u> but the sword; and Herod's men
> Steal through the valleys with their large knives drawn.

His mother shall arise before the day
And flee with him far out of Bethlehem,
And there, unknown and exiled, shall He stay,
The promised King who builds Jerusalem.

And when He shall return into His own,
Thy brethren shall spit upon His head,
And claim the pagan Caesar for the throne
And curse themselves, and shout to see Him dead.

But when through all the ages they shall sing
Of how the God of Heaven sent his Son,
And how the people did not know their King,—
Then shall they sing of thee, my little one.

Then shall they sing the Holy Innocents,
Who from bright Heaven, amongst the cherubim,
Beg Him to close His eyes to our offence,
Who have not known, who have not cherished Him.

The other one I think must have been a few verses of one about
our Lady's childhood:

How did she view our earth, that holy child, called down from
    Heaven by prayer, God's gift and prize,
Dressed with the loveliness of a timeless Eve and the young
    David's eyes?

With soul a glory, heart a guarded fire, she grew, oh,—beauty's
    self—unmarred by pain—
To her enchanted gaze our sodden earth was Paradise again.

> With my fondest love always—
> Julian

Talacre Abbey
Gronant
Prestatyn

22 Oct 1961

Dearest Noreen,

Your birthday this year is rather a special one for me, because it coincides with the 25th anniversary of my first Mass. I had hoped to spend the day at Stonor, but haven't been able to get rid of a very heavy cold, so I may even spend the day in bed!

Having seen a young mother, who spent four months at a farmhouse just above the Abbey this summer with her six months-old baby, I realize more than ever how completely engrossing they are and that you can't possibly ever have time for writing letters. But in any case I am sure that we have long ago said everything to each other that can possibly be said in letters, and that we no longer need them as proof of our feelings and of our frequent thoughts.

I also realize that babies are not people to be taken on journeys more than is absolutely necessary and that it may mean that I have to wait another year or two before I see you again, but it will only make it all the lovelier when I do, and of course it will be so thrilling to see Pam now that she has grown as lovely as you, to see your unchangingly perfect Johnny, to whom I am sure even the 6 foot 5 Nicky can't hold a candle yet when it comes to perfection of character, and to see the new and adorable Pussy Willow.

Knowing your ways, I am in the embarrassing position of being almost, but not absolutely, certain that you and Johnny are the "strictly anonymous" source of £100 for my silver jubilee towards getting a small second-hand car. If it is, I am, of course, most deeply grateful, because the bus and train services in North Wales are so bad and in any case I am twenty minutes walk from the only bus that comes anywhere near, so that I spend most of my time at bus stops at stations, which is probably where I get my succession of colds and bad ears. But I really hope most of all that it isn't you this time, because you both spend your whole lives giving, giving, giving, and now that you have your three children to think of in this fantastically expensive world, I would far rather think that you were having a rest from all your other givings, at any rate until Pam is safely married to someone who will care for her as lovingly as Johnny does you, and Nicky launched on whatever career he is going to take up.

With my fondest love to them all and to darling Julie—and may they all, together with your father and mother and Nadine, combine to give you a <u>wonderful</u> birthday to make up for all our worries this time last year.

Always your affectionate
Julian

Talacre Abbey
Gronant
20 Nov. 1961

Dearest Noreen,

I do hope that your mother is making as wonderful a recovery from her operation as your father did, and our own Nicky. Sherman sent me a telegram about a week ago, but I haven't heard anything since.

This morning I managed to extract a list out of Charles of the people who had had the wonderfully kind thought of commemorating my 25th anniversary last month with the gift of a chalice. And of course, as I might have known, the list was headed by you and Johnny. Bless you both for all your wonderful kindness and generosity, but above all for being what you <u>are</u>—the one absolutely perfect family that I am sure God has given us all as an inspiration. That darling Julia has, of course, loved the opportunity of seeing so much of you and says she now understands the special niche you hold in my heart.

The Dunalleys—the friends of mine we had lunch with at the little inn in Ireland—send you their love. Philippa, despite her polio, has just produced a second son, after nearly as long an interval as your lovely Pussy Willow. I hear Dromoland is for sale! With my fondest love to you all five—and of course to your mother and father as well.

Bless you always—Julian

Talacre
29.11.61

Darling Noreen,

Never dreaming that Johnny and Pam would face that winter crossing of the Atlantic to pay such a lovely tribute of gratitude to your mother, I had put off writing to you until I could tell you about her last laying to rest at Pishill, but now of course they will have been able to tell you far more, and I can concentrate on trying to help you to bear what must seem such an agonizing void in your life. Although I never saw your mother, Johnny gave me such a wonderful picture of her on Monday evening that I can begin to understand something of how you must miss her. And of course Our Lord understands what you are feeling even more.

I always think one of the loveliest of the things in the gospels is the fact that tears welled up into his eyes and trickled down his cheeks when he saw how bravely Martha and Mary Magdalen were trying to bear the agony of the loss of their only brother Lazarus (they were all unmarried and not much older than your Pam and Nicky), even though he knew in a few moments he was going to give Lazarus back to them. It was the knowledge of what they were suffering at that moment that moved him so deeply that he simply couldn't hold back the tears. He really will understand the moments of anguish you will keep having for a long time yet whenever your mother flashes into your mind.

On that occasion he gave them Lazarus back (though, of course, he took him from them again eventually), but chiefly to show us the fact that physical death, even with its attendant finality of the body being gradually transformed again into the dust out of which all earthly bodies are fashioned, whether of flowers or animals or human beings, means absolutely nothing in his sight and that he can clothe a soul again in its body whenever He wants to. When he whispered Talitha, cumi ('Darling, get up!') to the little 12-year-old daughter of Jainus [sic] or gave her only son back to the widow of Niam [sic], we might have thought that perhaps they hadn't really died, as it was only a matter of hours, but in the case of Lazarus, he deliberately waited for three days, in spite of the agony he knew it was causing to the two sisters, in order to convince us, and them, that real death, even with its physical corruption, was still completely under his control and power.

And when the time does come for Him to pluck each flower, just when He knows that it has reached the greatest perfection it will ever reach, His timing is always so absolutely exquisite. You remember how it was with my mother and sister, and, two days before your mother, He took our cousin, Violet Clifton. All her life she had had a tremendous devotion to that lovely Saint Elizabeth of Hungary; she had written the most wonderful life of her in poetry, just called 'Sanctity', which made a tremendous stir in England when it appeared, and, like Saint Elizabeth, God completed her perfection by allowing her to know the grief of widowhood and the joy of then giving up all her wealth (though she wasn't a Queen, Lytham Hall is far more magnificent than Stonor and the Cliftons have lived there just as long) and spending her last years alone with God in the poverty of a Poor Clare Franciscan convent. And the day He took her was November 19th, the feast of Saint Elizabeth.

And in your mother's case too, as you know, he couldn't have timed it more perfectly—waiting till the year when you would have Pussy Willow to console and distract you from your sadness and finally, after your mother had prepared herself in her own way for the possibility of her own death under the operation, setting her mind at rest again and then taking her very, very, suddenly before she could realize what had happened and without any of the often long-drawn-out process of dying which is needed by so many people to bring them to perfection. And, of course, His absolutely effortless omnipotence and providence ever foresees the lesser figures in the drama. If the funeral had been any other day, the Thoresens wouldn't have been able to show that almost unbelievable love for your mother's memory which Johnny will have told you about—reaching her gravesite in spite of a railway and every other kind of strike in France and a terrible gale in the Channel which held them up for hours and hours. Even my joy of being able to offer my Mass for her in the Stonor Chapel which you had restored and of kneeling by her body in the drawing room the night before wouldn't have been possible on any other day last week or this, as I have been completely booked up with lectures, prize givings, conferences, etc, and Tuesday morning was the only one on which my supply-priest would come.

But, of course, what I feel even more grateful for than the place of the Mass—for the place doesn't really matter in such things—was the unforgettable joy of hearing Johnny talk about your mother, and poor Sherman too (who looked <u>so</u> old and sad), who said that <u>everything</u> he had learnt about praying and about Our Lord's goodness he had learnt from <u>her</u>. And although I know you would have loved her to be buried near you, in Newport, I <u>do</u> think it was what God wanted that she should be buried among all the family at Stonor, because when the full story is complete, perhaps in hundreds of years' time, she will have played such a wonderful part in it. As you know, the Stonors are terribly reserved and shy—you only have to think of Aunt Julie or Francis or Charles—and find it terribly hard to show any affection they may feel—but the infusion of deep love and affection that she has bequeathed so strongly to you and Sherman will go on multiplying through each generation, as it has already done in all your children and all Sherman's.

I simply can't tell you how overwhelmed I was by Pam. I never dreamt that anybody could be as lovely as you, but she really is. She is just like what I am sure people are going to be like in Heaven. It made one feel holy just being near her. I wish I could write more, but if I do, it will never go by air.

With all my deepest love—Julian

Talacre Abbey
11.12.61

Dearest Noreen,

I do hope that by now you will be beginning to <u>feel</u> and <u>know</u> that your Mother is looking after you just as unceasingly as she did before, in fact far more so, as she no longer needs the sleep that an earthly body needs, and without any of the anxiety which marred it both for herself and for you while she was on earth.

I meant to tell Johnny, but we were interrupted, about one of my second-sight glimpses which I think will show you what I mean.

One night in Liverpool I was reading in bed about two in the morning—a book about Cumberland—when I suddenly knew that a man had just been killed at a cross-roads outside Marlborough (in Wiltshire). I had even met him—his name was Myron Tuchak, a Jewish pilot, but, years ago, I had met his wife once or twice—she was an Irish girl who rode beautifully, and the second time, she had mentioned that she was going to marry this pilot and had asked me about the religious side, as he was a practicing Jew. They lived at Walton-on-Thames near London airport, and he flew planes across the Atlantic to Canada.

As soon as he was killed, he seemed to be begging me to help his wife, Eileen, and to tell her how fond he was of her (I didn't know that she had just had their first baby). I wrote to her that morning and it was only through my letter that she found out what had happened. Owing to bad weather he had landed at Bristol and persuaded another pilot to swap duties with him and lend him his car. And it was in that car that he was killed at two that morning, so that when the police found him, they couldn't identify him and presumed it was someone who had stolen the car of this other pilot, who had by then flown to Canada.

I didn't actually <u>see</u> him on this occasion,—in fact I still don't know what he looked like—but what I <u>did</u> feel, and what I am sure is equally true of your mother, was the tremendous strength of his love for his wife and the touching way in which his very first thought after his death was to get in touch with the only priest whom he knew she trusted and would believe.

With my fondest love to you all
Julian

Downside Abbey
27.1.62

Dearest Noreen,

At last I have escaped from hospital and have been able to get hold of some air-mail paper and find the number of your Box at Hobe Sound from my address book. I couldn't ask for the paper in the hospital, as part of the treatment was six weeks complete rest with no letter-writing.

I feel miles better after it and find it very hard to believe that I won't be able to climb any stairs or do anything energetic for several months yet. But I am still hoping to return to Talacre about the end of March, and have been promised a small car, which will make a tremendous difference to life there. Sherman & Jeanne are, of course, bringing great pressure to bear on the Abbot to send me to Stonor instead—Jeanne is driving over to see him on Monday—but, apart from anything else, I really do feel that dealing with all the parties and pilgrimages would be too much for me now and it would mean an enormous correspondence on top of my own. After spending Christmas in hospital—I have over 400 letters and parcels waiting to be answered!

But, of course, the most wonderful news of all is that you may be coming over this summer. I don't think I would be able to get away again after being away for four months, but I am sure you would love Wales just as much as Ireland. Some of it is just as wild and lovely as Connemara.

I will write again as soon as I have arrived at wherever it is decided that I do my convalescence.

With my fondest love to all five of you and <u>longing</u> to see you—
Julian

Caldy Manor
24 April 1962

Dearest Noreen,

Your lovely letter and photographs arrived this morning—
together with the first real day of spring! I <u>love</u> the one of the three
children together, but, most of all, the close-up of Pussy Willow on
the swing. It is such an enchantingly innocent little face and yet so
bursting with intelligence and character.

And I can see a distinct likeness to your father in her—and
an even greater likeness to a photograph I was sent recently of
Archbishop Stonor!!

I can still hardly believe that I will be seeing you in only a
matter of a few weeks.

The doctor has just told me that I can definitely go to Stonor
on any day after May 1st—and that, after three months' holiday,
he agrees with the Abbot (and me!) that Talacre is far and away
the best place for me to spend the next two years in real peace
and quiet. I have been given a Rover car, which will cut out the
steep hills there, which were the only drawback.

I am so glad now that it is not <u>this</u> summer that you are all
coming over to Ireland and Europe, because the doctor has banned
any travelling for me for this summer, and I would so love to see
Ireland again with you all.

I haven't heard yet when Julie is expected home, but I do hope
it is while you are over here.

I feel so guilty about all the sympathy I have been getting,
because I have really loved every minute of these five months
and have almost decided to get a coronary at the beginning of
every winter!

With all my fondest love to each of the five of you, and of course
to your father when you go back to New York—and <u>longing</u> to
see you—

Julian

Talacre Abbey
Gronant
Prestatyn
N. Wales

6 October 1962

My darling Noreen,

As always seems to happen to me, dear Johnny's birthday has caught up with me too late for a letter—and I am so terrified that the same will happen with you.

[It nearly has, for it is now the 12th and I don't see much hope of getting any real time to myself for at least ten days after that because there is still a steady stream of people coming out to see me now that the word has spread that I am back.]

I really did love my four months at Stonor. Sherman was <u>so</u> kind, though he is terribly unhappy about the possibility of a rift with you and Johnny, the two people whom he loves and admires most in the world. And he has never felt more unhappy about not being able to write to either of you, now that he has the additional anxiety of your father's new decision.

And though it was so sad not having Julie at home—and Thomas and Georgina away most of the time—it was lovely really getting to know Harriet again, who is such a thoughtful unselfish character. I suspect that you have heard that she is now in the same nursing home where I was, suffering from a terrible stone in the kidneys. But I believe the worst is over for her, but she is so frail, and weighs less than 6 stone.

While I was there, I completely rewrote the family history from beginning to end—there won't be a single paragraph the same—I had never realized how dreadful the old book was, and I hope you will find the new one far more readable—I have also brought it up to date—including little bits about Pam and Nicky.

I am so glad you have that adorable Pussy Willow to comfort you during this sad period, and I am still hoping to see her next summer. I really do feel much, much, better and I have this Ford car which makes life much easier and—what I love even more, I have been lent a lovely 17-hands black horse, with the most charming manners. I haven't actually been allowed to ride him yet, but queues of nurses and other friends come out to do so!

I do hope you will have a very happy birthday and that God will guide you in everything you do, so that you will always be loved more and more by everyone, though I am sure you will never be loved by anyone more than by me.

With <u>all</u> my love always—
Julian

ILLUSTRATIONS

Father Julian Stonor

Noreen Stonor Drexel greeting President and Mrs. John F. Kennedy

Noreen at ease

*Portrait of Noreen Stonor Drexel
by René Bouché*

*Stonor Cousins: Pam and Nicky Drexel (L), Thomas
(today Lord Camoys) and Georgina Stonor (R).*

Stonor Chapel

St Mary's
Highfield St
Liverpool 3

24. August.

Dearest Noreen –

For once my luck deserted me yesterday and I got to the Pitty just five minutes after you had all left for Cornwall. Still, it was wonderful to know that Johnny was well enough to undertake the journey, and of course the thought of your visit here on my Birthday has made me deliriously happy.

I was on my way to a Requiem Mass for Sir John Reynolds – a very old friend of mine – and had called in at Stour for an hour the evening before. Unfortunately I just missed Sherman, and Harriet and Charles

But Jeanne and the other children were really very nice.

An Irish Guards Colonel, another great friend of Jack Reynolds, had met me in Oxford and was driving me down to his house at Southampton for the night and I had been hoping to spend the rest of yesterday with you all; as I hadn't then received your letter. But I am so glad that you have all been able to see Molly, and only hope the journey wasn't too much of an agony for poor Johnny.

The parish priest got back yesterday, but is off again on Monday, so I will be on full duty on the 28th, I am afraid, but Tuesday is nearly always the least busy day of the week.

Thank you very, very much for such a sweet thought. With my fondest love to you all —

Julian

St Mary's
Liverpool
Christmas Eve.

Dearest Noreen –

All your letters arrived today,
including a really <u>lovely</u> card from
darling Pam, which sent my hopes
rocketing up for a few moments
when I saw it had a Belgian stamp
on it.

I myself am feeling rather
forlorn this Christmas, because none
of my own cards will reach
anybody in time for Christmas, and
yours (which, of course, matters to me
most) probably not till the Epiphany,
as I don't know your address in
Florida.

For the last fortnight or so I
have been working at higher pressure
than ever before in my life, but it
has all been intermingled with such
a fantastic series of the most wonderful
experiences (one of them, I think, really
miraculous) — most of them deaths,
including, at last, my dear little Josie,
but some of them quite amazing conversions —
that it has had a wonderfully calming
effect on me.   Although one thing follows
another in an unending stream for 19 or 20
hours a day, and half the things completely
unexpected and unplanned, God's timing
of them has been so unbelievably
accurate (to the very minute in almost
every case) that it has brought a
great sense of peace and of certainty
as to God's providence). The only thing
which has suffered has been my
Christmas mail.

I wish I could tell you about some of the things, but it would take too long, so I will wait till I see you; because I must try and write as many letters as I can tonight.

I felt rather guilty about my last depressed letter written when Eden seemed bent on plunging us into another world war; but, thank Heaven, we very soon began shifting back on to the side of law and order; though, alas!, it completely sapped our moral strength, just when Hungary needed all our moral support.

There was a horrid period when the guilty people here tried to pin the blame on America, but the verdict of history will obviously be that America upheld the western ideals magnificently throughout.

Your darling Pam wrote me a sweet letter from school last term, and this term I am determined to write her one — and Nicky too. Do please thank them both for their lovely cards. It was so like them to take such trouble that their greetings should reach me over all those thousands of miles that separate us — and not a word, alas, from anybody at Stonor.

With my fondest love and blessings to you all four, and I will be thinking of you so often during these next days - at Newport, in New York and in Florida —

Julian

POST CARD

Communication | Address

The eye has made an almost
complete recovery since yesterday
so that I am out and about
again; and yesterday evening
was able to hire a horse at a
country-house hotel near here
and ride up to visit some farms
right up in the hills, near where this
photograph was taken – the loveliest
evening I have had since your visit
in the summer. Love to you all.
Greetings from   J.

The Hon. Mrs John Drexel

Merrymount

Newport

Rhode Island

U. S. A.

St. Mary's

TANTUM

ERGO

Highfield St.
Liverpool

Tantum ergo sacramentum
Veneremur cernui ;
Et antiquum documentum
Novo cedat ritui ;
Praestet fides supplementum
Sensuum defectui.

Genitori, Genitoque
Laus et jubilatio
Salus, honor, virtus, quoque
Sit et benedictio ;
Procedenti ab utroque
Compar sit laudatio. Amen.

Mid-day

Services

DURING LENT, 1956

**All are requested to join in the
singing**

Please Keep This Programme

James Kilburn, *Printer*,
59a, Russell St., Liverpool 3

ST. MARY'S, HIGHFIELD STREET, LIVERPOOL, 3

Mid-day Lenten Services, 1956

Each **Week-day** (except Saturday) between the First Sunday of Lent and
Palm Sunday from **12.30—12.55 p.m.**
The Service will consist of **Sermon** and **Short Benediction**

General Title of the Series of Sermons—

" THAT CHRIST MAY DWELL BY FAITH IN YOUR HEARTS "

Eph. III, 17

1st Week — Commencing Monday, 20th February :—
Preacher : DOM HUBERT VAN-ZELLER, O.S.B.
" THAT YOU MAY BE ABLE TO COMPREHEND, WITH ALL THE SAINTS, WHAT
IS THE BREADTH AND LENGTH AND DEPTH AND HEIGHT." Ephesians III, 18.
Is Personal Communion with God possible ? How does it help anyone
else ? The way to God which turns ordinary duties into Acts of Prayer.

2nd Week — Commencing Monday, 27th February :—
Preacher : REV. HAROLD CRAIG, S.J.
" CHRIST — THE LIFE OF THE SOUL."
1. Christ Our Only Way (means of Salvation) ; 2, Christ Our Life ;
3, Christ Our Friend ; 4, Christ Our King ; 5, Christ Our Judge.

3rd Week — Commencing Monday, 5th March :—
Preacher : DOM JULIAN STONOR, O.S.B.
" CHRIST — OUR REDEEMER "
The Lamb of God—The Central Figure of The Old Testament and The
New, of the Church on Earth and in Heaven.

4th Week — Commencing Monday, 12th March :—
Preacher : VERY REV. DOMINIC DEVAS, O.F.M.
" THE MASS — LET NO ONE SAY THAT THIS HAS NOTHING TO DO WITH OUR
SANCTIFICATION."
Jesus Himself whole and entire, is our Food ; His Body, His Blood, His
Soul, His Divinity. He is united to us to Transform us into Himself.

5th Week — Commencing Monday, 19th March :—
" MAY YOU BE FILLED WITH ALL THE COMPLETION GOD HAS TO GIVE."
Ephesians III, 19.

THIS LAST WEEK IS **YOUR** MISSION

Conducted by : VERY REV. GEORGE P. DWYER, C.M.S.

GENERAL COMMUNION — FRIDAY, 23rd MARCH — 5-30 p.m. MASS

The Vladimir Mother of God

Best loved of ancient Russian ikons now hangs in the Tretiakov Museum, Moscow. Widely venerated in the East and symbolising the hope and trust of all Christians, Our Lady of Vladimir may yet draw East and West together in peace. Such a gesture of Christian friendship inspired the making of this card.

Noreen —

With all my love
&
Best wishes for
Christmas
and the coming year

from

Julian

Sponsored by the Sodalities
of Our Lady

R & T Washbourne   London

Our Lady of Vladimir

SERMONS

INTRODUCTION

"I HAVE LIFTED UP MY EYES TO THE MOUNTAINS, from whence help will come to me.... The high places of the mountains God himself looks upon".

These words of King David are not mere poetry, for it is historically true that mountain-peaks and hill-tops have provided the scene for all the supreme moments in the story of God's wooing of his wayward human race; we have but to think of the summits of Mount Horeb in Sinai and Mount Nebo, of Mount Ephraim and Mount Carmel, of Mount Hermon and Mount Tabor and, as the center of the story in both Old and New Covenants, Mount Moriah, on whose summit lay the little town of Jerusalem and the hill of Calvary. Even in the Christian centuries it has often been the same, and we think at once of Saint Patrick passing Lent on the summit of Croaghpatrick, of Saint Benedict on Monte Cassino or of Saint Francis spending forty days and nights on Mount Alvernia.

It was the summit of Mount Horeb in the desert of Sinai which God chose for the supreme revelation of himself to the two greatest figures in the Old Testament—Moses and Elias [Elijah]. The greatness of Moses's work has often blinded people to the gentleness and loveableness of his character. The Bible tells us that "Moses was a man exceeding meek among all men that dwelt upon earth", and he was a faithful prototype of Our Lord too in his desire to take upon himself all the sinfulness and ingratitude of God's people—again and again his prayer was to be "Father, forgive them, for they know not what they do". This Moses often spent long periods of solitude up in Mount Horeb during the many years which the children of Israel spent encamped at its foot. It was after he had been up there alone, fasting and in silence, for forty days, that he received those Ten Commandments which, as the double commandment of love—"Thou shalt love the Lord thy God with thy whole heart and with thy whole soul and with thy whole mind and with all thy strength; and thou shalt love thy neighbour as thyself"—have been the basis of all morality ever since and which transformed those poor idolatrous slaves from Egypt, whose fathers had been so dazzled by the stupendous pagan temples among which they had dwelt, into the People of God.

185

We have Moses's own description of the revelation which God made to him on that occasion of that overwhelming love which is the essence of the divine nature and which is more than unaided human nature can bear—how God made known to him: "Thou canst not see my face, for man cannot see me and live, but behold...thou shalt stand upon a rock and when my glory shall pass I will set thee in a hole of the rock and protect thee with my right hand till I have passed, and then I will take away my hand and thou shalt see my back, but my face thou canst not see...And when the Lord was come down Moses stood with him, calling upon the name of the Lord, and as the Lord passed before him he said: O Lord, the Lord God, gracious and full of pity, patient and of great compassion and true, who keepest mercy unto thousands and who takest away iniquity and wickedness and sin... And Moses, making haste, bowed down prostrate to the ground and, adoring, said: O Lord, I beseech thee that thou wilt go with us and take away our iniquities and sin and possess us". Ever after that experience there was such holiness reflected in Moses's own face that the children of Israel could not bear to look upon it.

And it was to this same mountain-top of Horeb, where the covenant of love between God and his people was made through Moses, that Elias came when, after six hundred years, Moses's great work of making God's love known to men seemed finally to be crashing into ruin and idolatry again triumphant. He too had been fasting for forty days and nights when he climbed the mountain. "And when he was come thither he abode in a cave, and behold the word of the Lord came to him: What dost thou here, Elias? And he answered: With zeal I have been zealous for the Lord God of Hosts, for the children of Israel have forsaken thy covenant, they have thrown down thy altars, they have slain thy prophets with the sword, and I alone am left and they seek my life to take it away. And God said to him: Go forth and stand upon the mountain before the Lord, and behold the Lord passeth, and a great and strong wind before the Lord...the Lord is not in the wind, and after the wind an earthquake, the Lord is not in the earthquake, and after the earthquake a fire, the Lord is not in the fire, and after the fire a whistling of a gentle air...and when Elias heard it, he covered his face with his mantle".

When we remember too that Our Lord himself deliberately spent forty days in fasting and complete solitude in the mountains before beginning his task of revealing to men the greatness of their Father's love, and that in the subsequent months he went frequently to the silence of the mountain-tops, we realize the important part that such periods of silence must play in our spiritual life of drawing near to God while we are on earth and so much at the mercy of the multitudinous distractions which are always crowding in upon us through our senses. Saint John of the Cross used to make his novices spend whole days alone among the flowers and the birds in the sunshine as the best way to come to understand God's love, just as Saint Francis did. If in times of retreat and prayer you are always either saying vocal prayers or listening to someone else's words in sermons or books, it means that your soul is really keeping up a jabber of conversation in God's presence, whereas even a few minutes of silent realization of God's love are much more precious both to him and to you than many hours of wearying yourself out by talking to him or about him all the time so that he cannot get a word in edgeways.

That, surely, is the significance of the whistling of the gentle air which ushered in the supreme moment of revelation to Elias. God's revelation of himself to us is so infinitely more important than anything we can say to him. What we should pray for in a retreat is that while we sit at Our Lord's feet with Mary of Bethany in silent adoration and love, he may lift the veil for us and enable us to see this life in a truer perspective. You will remember that incident in the life of Eliseus [Elisha] when his servant came to him in his cave on Mount Carmel and, in a state of great alarm, told him that the mountain was surrounded by soldiers who had come to arrest him; Eliseus answered: "Fear not, for there are more with us than with them". And then, seeing that the servant was obviously not much comforted by that answer, he prayed and said: "Lord, open his eyes that he may see". And the Lord opened the eyes of the servant and he saw, and behold the mountain was full of chariots and horses of fire round about Eliseus.

For us, even more than for Eliseus (who desired to hear the things that we have heard, but did not hear them), there should always be that vision of the real world, compared to which the life which to so many others seems the only real and important one is as <u>un</u>real as a cinema film. But to see things as they really are does <u>not</u> mean that we will not enjoy the passing film of this life as much as those other people. On the contrary, we will enjoy it far, far more. Those who have to base all their hopes and ambitions on the passing illusions of this film-like life are the ones we ought to feel sorry for, because the reel flashes past relentlessly from the irrevocable past, through the instantaneous present—which is gone without our being able to hold it for a moment—to a future which is ever growing shorter and shorter. They may keep up the struggle for a time and hope for other pleasures to take the place of those which have flashed past beyond recall, but soon they know in their heart of hearts that it is a losing battle, until, finally, they begin to realize that the last reel of the film must have begun and that very soon it will all be over, and, as far as they know, their own existence will end with it.

But we, who have the privilege of knowing all the time that it is only a film, not only enjoy the picture itself all the more—because we see and feel all the lovely things that they do, only with the added joy of knowing that they have been made specially for us by someone who loves us, while at the same time, unlike them, we know that the moments of sadness and suffering are only there to increase our love, like a mother hiding sometimes from her small child so that it may prove its love by feeling unhappy without her and wanting her and so that she may give it the joy of finding her again—but, besides having a deeper joy while the film lasts, we have the greatest source of joy of all in knowing that, as soon as it is over, we are going out into a far more beautiful and wonderful world than can ever be shown on the screen. "For eye hath not seen, nor ear heard, neither hath it entered into the heart of men to conceive what things God hath prepared for them that love him".

And so, both for your own sakes and for the sake of the more short-sighted people whom you will often be meeting, remember that you cannot be too happy. The more you radiate joy and love, the more God will love you for it—and the more you will, perhaps unconsciously, enable other people to see him more clearly. Does any earthly parent want to see its child always crying and fretting and unhappy? And remember that God is pure untrammelled Love, multiplied to infinity beyond any love which we can possibly conceive, that his only reason for making us was that we might be happy and realize his love, and that all the lovely things in this life were made for us and for us alone—from the warmth of the sun down to the taste of every strawberry which we eat. It is only in non-Catholic countries that you normally find gloomy faces, preoccupied with money and politics, and religion associated with black clothes and drawn blinds on Sundays and teetotalism. Wherever you find Catholic culture undisturbed, there you find happiness and joy, music and song and clothes of the brightest colors which man can make—almost as bright as the colors with which God has clothed this temporary world for us.

I

The Flashing Lights in the Sky

SOMETIME AFTER THE COVENANT OF LOVE
between God and his chosen people had been made known to
Moses on Mount Horeb, he began to write down for the children
of Israel the story of God's love for them. Those forty thousand
fighting-men who, with their wives and children, had grown up
during the forty years in the desert of Sinai, must often have
wondered, as they sat round their campfires in the evenings or lay
on the sand at night under the heavens ablaze with stars, about
the nature of this world in which they themselves seemed so
insignificant. And so Moses began by describing how this great
visible world came into existence.

The dividing of time into periods of seven days, with the seventh day as a day of rest, had already been held sacred by their
ancestors for five hundred years, because Abraham had brought
it with him from Mesopotamia (that is why the wording of the
commandment had been: "Remember the seventh day, to keep it
holy"). And so when Moses wanted to teach them, in a form of
poetry, to memorize the different stages in the world's evolution,
he specified six stages or days, followed by a day of rest. (The Papal
Commission for Biblical Studies has pronounced definitely that the
Hebrew word "yom", used by Moses, may be taken as meaning any
period of time, however long). Actually, he only really described
three stages, for he simply took first the three basic materials out
of which the whole world has been made and then the three great
groups of things which were fashioned out of those materials.

The first of the three materials is, of course, light, because,
radically, the whole visible world is just a collection of huge lights,
though some of the smaller ones have now gone out, as has the
one on which we are living at present. Then the second material is
the watery space in which these lights are set and which, as viewed
from our earth, is quite rightly divided into the upper firmament,
in which the stars move, and the more condensed lower firmament,
the blanket of moist atmosphere surrounding our earth, which we
are able to breathe and which moves round with the earth and

thus prevents us being swept off of it, and, most condensed of all, the huge pools of water which gathered on the earth's surface as it began to grow cool and which the fishes breathe. And, finally, there is the third material, the <u>dry ground with its vegetation,</u> which also resulted from the quenching of the fires of the earth.

Then, having described the three materials which God created, he goes back and describes the three great armies of moving things which God made out of those materials. "<u>So the heavens and the earth were finished and all the armies of them</u>" is the literal translation of the Hebrew of Genesis 2:1. That is why it is only to the fourth day that he assigns the creation of the sun and the moon and the stars—not that he thought that there was any created light before them or that there could be what we call a day before the creation of the sun and the earth. Then, commemorated on the fifth day is the creation of the fishes and the birds and the great prehistoric reptiles to move in the lower firmament of the water or the watery atmosphere. And, finally on the sixth day, animals and men to dwell on the face of the earth and eat its fruits. It is all described so simply, and yet the greatest scientist would not be able to find a single thing which is not included in Moses's few simple sentences or to suggest a more plausible ordering of the events. Thereafter the same order continually occurs in Hebrew literature, descending from the vast depths of space through the moist atmosphere in its different forms to the earth with its vegetation and its ascending evolution of animal life culminating in men. We have but to think of the Song of the Three Children in the fiery furnace—

O ye heavens, bless the Lord...
O ye stars of heaven, bless the Lord...
O ye rain and dew, bless the Lord...
O let the earth bless the Lord...
O all ye things that germinate in the earth, bless the Lord...
O ye whales and all that move in the waters, bless the Lord...
O all ye birds of the air, bless the Lord...
O all ye beasts and cattle, bless the Lord...
O ye sons of men, bless the Lord...

And since it was only for the sons of men during their passing life on the earth that all this was made, we surely have a duty to stop and think about these things sometimes and allow our senses also to dwell in gratitude on some of the sheer loveliness which God has lavished upon us so extravagantly and so needlessly. Indeed we have Our Lord's own express words urging us to do so: "Consider the birds of the air... how your heavenly father feedeth them.... Consider the flowers of the field... for if the grass of the field, which is today and tomorrow is cast into the oven, God so clothes, how much more ye, o ye of little faith?" There are so many riches—from the mightiest nebula blazing in the sky to the tiny little blue butterfly sunning itself on a stone—that one cannot talk about them all, but one can only indicate some of the beauties in the three different groups.

First, then, the stars. "And God said: Let there be light... And God said: Let there be lights made in the firmament of heaven... to shine in the firmament of heaven and to give light upon the earth" (first and fourth "days"). No people in the East, where the night air is so clear that the whole sky seems to be a vast shimmering sea of flashing lights, have ever taken the stars so casually as we do, who scarcely give a thought to their existence. Sometimes by Babylonians and Assyrians they were thought to be gods or demons; but the children of Israel were never to forget the warning contained in Moses's last blessing from the slopes of Mount Nebo, after he had viewed the Promised Land which he himself might not enter: "In the wilderness, as thou hast seen, the LORD thy God hath carried thee, as a man is wont to carry his little son, all the way that you have come to this place... neither is there any other nation so great that hath gods so nigh them as our God is present to all our petitions. Keep therefore your souls carefully... lest perhaps lifting up thy eyes to heaven thou see the sun and the moon and all the stars of heaven and, being deceived by error, thou adore and serve them, which the LORD thy God created for the service of all the nations that are under heaven". And so in after years when they looked up to the night sky, it set them thinking only of the greatness of God who had made it all—

> O Israel, how great is the house of God and how vast
> is the place of his possession! It is great and hath no
> end, high and immense.

He sends forth the light and it goeth. He calleth it and it obeyeth him with trembling. The stars have given light in their watches and have rejoiced; they were called and they said: We are here; and with cheerfulness they shone forth to him who made them.

He stretched out the north over the empty space and hangeth the earth upon nothing...till light and darkness come to an end, the pillars of heaven tremble and dread at his beck.... His spirit hath adorned the heavens.... Where wast thou when I laid the foundations of the earth...when the morning stars praised me together?... Shalt thou be able to join together the shining stars, the Pleiades, or canst thou stop the turning about of Arcturus? Canst thou bring forth the day star in its time and make the evening star to rise above the children of the earth?

When I consider thy heavens, the work of thy hands, the moon and stars which thou hast made, what is man that thou art mindful of him, or the son of man that thou visitest him?

The whole world before thee is as the least grain of a balance and as a drop of the morning dew that falleth down upon the earth.

Our telescopes allow us to see further than the Hebrews could even imagine into that vast array of lights through which our little planet is circling. We can now see so far out into the depths of space that we can make out that those millions of great fires which we can see burning there are arranged in gigantic patterns—known as island universes—circling round like enormous Catherine Wheels, and that our planet is on the outer rim of one of those wheels—a wheel which we are looking at from the rim when we gaze at the Milky Way stretching across the sky. The other island universes are all speeding away from us, and astronomers seem puzzled because there appears to be a fixed rule that the further they are away the faster they are travelling—the speed of the nearest being twenty miles a second and that of the furthest sixty thousand miles a second, which is a third as fast as the speed at which light itself flashes through the darkness. Yet the answer is so simple, if only they could see it. For if they all started off millions of years ago near enough for their light to have reached us by now—and otherwise we would not be seeing them at all—and if they are all moving at different speeds, it is only natural that by now the fastest-moving ones should be the furthest away.

Another thing which brings home to us how the stars were made only for us is the age of the individual stars which make up these gigantic patterns. For we can see them burning away to extinction before our eyes. Not only was it necessary for each one of those myriads of great fires to have begun to burn at a date which would enable its light to reach us (which often takes many thousands of years) by the time we were created to see it, but also we can see that they all began to burn at roughly the same time—at that time when God said: "Let there be light". For it is only the difference in their sizes which accounts for the differing stages which they have reached now. Some of the mightiest ones are still burning with such an intense heat that they give out a white, almost bluish-white, light, but the majority, like our own sun, are now surrounded by clouds of carbon vapor which cause them to give a yellowish light, while the smaller ones have become surrounded by such dense clouds as they burn out that they cannot be seen by the naked eye, and, finally, we have the dark extinguished fragments, like our own earth or the moon, which are only lit by a neighboring light.

The time will come when the whole of this sudden conflagration will have been quenched. If God had said "Let there be light" a few million years earlier, the whole conflagration would have been over before we were created. But in the design of God's providence we are living at the unique stage, which can never occur again, when all the stars are alight together, so that they fill the sky for us as thickly as buttercups a meadow. And vast as their ages seem to us, who are only on this earth for about seventy years, yet in retrospect it will one day seem to us to have all been no more than a flash in the pan, and when the last of those mighty furnaces has smoldered into darkness forever, each one of our spirits will still have an eternity of life before it where he who in the beginning made heaven and earth shall say: "Behold I make all things new".

Nor should their size terrify us any more than their age. Not only is the intelligence which looks out through the astronomer's eye, as he examines the starry constellations with the instruments he has designed, far more wonderful than the great balls of fire which he sees, but so is the wonder of a small child who claps his hands with glee when he sees the stars glittering through the window. For it is but one of the wonderful gifts with which God has endowed the spirit that

> [W]e who are borne on one dark grain of dust
> Around one indistinguishable spark
> Of star-mist, lost in one lost feather of light,
> Can, by the strength of our own thought, ascend
> Through universe after universe, trace their growth
> Through boundless time, their glory, their decay.
>   (Alfred Noyes: "Watchers of the Sky")

II

Birds That Have Never Left the Sea

THE CREATION OF THE GREAT LIGHTS OCCUPIES
the first and the fourth days of Moses's scheme. The second
and the fifth days are concerned with the waters and the watery
atmosphere and those creatures which inhabit them.

"And God said: Let the waters that are under the heavens be
gathered together" (second day).

"And God also said: Let the waters bring forth the creeping
creature having life and the bird that may fly over the earth under
the firmament of heaven" (fifth day).

According to the Nebular Theory, the earth required a long time
in which to cool down to the temperature at which living matter
could exist upon it, and during that long period when it was void
of all living things it must have been surrounded by dense clouds
of vapor, afterward to condense into the oceans and the seas and
the great lakes. And according to the Theory of Evolution (which,
incidentally, was debated by the greatest thinkers of the Church
many centuries before Darwin and accepted in outline by Saint
Augustine and Saint Thomas Aquinas among others) animal life
did indeed originate in the warm waters which covered most of
the cooling earth.

"And God created the great whales and every living and moving
creature which the waters brought forth, according to their kinds,
and every winged fowl according to its kind. And He blessed them,
saying: Increase and multiply and fill the waters of the sea; and
let the birds be multiplied upon the earth".

Science agrees that gigantic saurians—the Brontosaurus, Pleio-
saurus, et cetera—(the word translated by "whales" could describe
these) were a remarkable feature of that early period, and there
are still today many more millions of birds which have never left
their birthplace in the sea than have "multiplied upon the earth".
When we see a chicken or a canary or a parrot, we do not think
at once: "There is a fish with wings"—if anything, we think of it
as an animal with wings. Yet modern science, and especially the
study of fossils, has proved that Moses was perfectly right, and

if you were to sail in a boat from the west coast of Ireland to go across to America, as you sailed further and further out into the ocean, you would see the birds belonging ever more completely to their place of origin in the waters, and it is among those that the wonder of God's providence in feeding them is most movingly shown.

On the first day out there would be the ordinary seagulls following in the wake of the ship, but by evening they would have dropped astern, and you might see others, which had been following other ships, flying back to the mainland from further out to sea. For, although we always think of the seagull as the typical sea-bird, it is really the most tied to land of them all; for it always sleeps on land and must have fresh water to drink, and indeed thousands of them have practically become land-birds, following the plough and scavenging near lakes and rivers.

The next morning the ship will still be over what is called the Continental Shelf, within soundings of a hundred fathoms. There may be a gull or two come out since dawn, but otherwise this comparatively shallow part of the ocean is the home of two groups of diving birds, innumerable in quantity, many of which spend their whole lives out here. The heavier divers, such as cormorants and gannets, which are as heavy as geese, drop like lumps of lead from about the height of the masthead to catch the herrings and mackerel which they can see from that height swimming about twenty or thirty feet beneath the surface. And the lighter divers, such as penguins and puffins and the diving ducks, swim on the surface most of the time, suddenly disappearing to chase and catch under water the smaller fish which swim just beneath the surface. These diving birds sleep on the sea. Their legs are developed enough to enable them to stand upright on rocks or icebergs, but their feet are webbed and are really fins for swimming under water, as are their small wings which, in the case of the swimming divers, are not strong enough to lift them off the level ground. That is why when they do come to land to nest it is always to the high cliffs, where they have only to tumble off their ledge in order to become airborne. (Perhaps "tumble" is not always the right word, for the preliminary mental anguish which the gannet appears to go through would make it a suitable emblem for a training unit for parachutists. There is a lot of shuffling about from one big webbed foot to the other, then it stretches out its neck skyward just as if it were praying and, at last, utters a low moan and jumps out into space.)

When the ship has at last left the fishing grounds of the Continental Shelf and is right out over the deep waters of the ocean, she enters the domain of the gliders—myriads and myriads of fascinating creatures, ranging in size from the mighty albatross, the largest of all birds, to the tiny little storm petrel, no bigger than a swallow. All through the year, through long months of Arctic twilight in the summer and through the blinding gales of rain and snow in the dark winter months of almost perpetual night, they glide tirelessly on stiff straight wings just above the surface of the cold heaving waters, buoyed up by the upward current of air that blows off the windward side of every wave. Their food is the floating harvest of minute animal and vegetable life, which is hatched out in vast quantities in the Arctic regions during the prolonged daylight of the summer months. These gliders are so like flying fish that many of them are unable even to stand upright on land; but, for a few weeks each year, they too, by some uncanny power of navigation, find their way across hundreds of miles of seemingly endless waves to some tiny rocky island, which one would have thought they might fly forever without finding.

During those few weeks in the summer, when every available foothold on the cliff faces is crowded by these divers and gliders, gathered from every part of the ocean, an amazing drama of God's providence takes place. To begin with, they are provided with eggs which are very thick at one end and very pointed at the other, for otherwise they would be swept off the narrow ledges by the thousand. But something more wonderful is to come. No instinct is stronger in any animal than that which urges a mother to satisfy the hunger of its young while it is still helpless; yet here that instinct would lead to disaster, for there are so many small fish in the sea at that time while the herrings and mackerel are spawning round the coast that the parent birds stuff those clamorous little balls of golden down almost to bursting point and, if this went on, as soon as the young birds attempted to reach the sea with their full bodies and undeveloped wings, they would fall headlong and be dashed to pieces on the rocks. But, one after another, the parents desert them and slip away to sea, never to see them again, and for the next week or two, while the flight feathers of the young birds are growing stronger and their bodies thinner, the cliffs resound with indignant cries of hunger. At last, when little more than clumps of feathers, they can bear it no longer and flutter over the edge, to glide safely to the sea below. There it at once becomes clear that this new element is their natural home, for the divers begin straightway washing and preening themselves, sipping the water and swimming and diving with ease, while the little storm petrels, instead of alighting on the water, are already skimming the surface like swallows, until, very soon, the spirit within each tiny warm body drives it to make its way alone out over the cold grey waters of the Atlantic. Never can it come home to one more poignantly, when one is holding one of those tiny living bundles in one's hand before it leaves its nest to begin its amazing life alone in a world of apparently barren sea-water, how much is implied in that word of Our Lord's: "Consider the birds of the air, how your heavenly Father feedeth them".

The Children for Whom the Nursery Is Adorned

"AND GOD CALLED THE DRY LAND EARTH AND God saw that it was good, and he said: Let the earth bring forth the green herb and such as may seed and the fruit tree yielding fruit after its kind". (third day)

"And God said: Let the earth bring forth the living creature in its kind, cattle and creeping things and beasts of the earth according to their kinds.... And he said: Let us make man to our image and likeness and let him have dominion over the fishes of the sea and the birds of the air and the beasts of the whole earth and every creeping creature that moves upon the earth.... And the LORD God formed man of the slime of the earth, and breathed into his face the breath of life and man became a living soul". (sixth day)

We have gazed from afar at those millions of flaming suns moving in dazzling array upon their ordered courses in the depths of space. And we have glanced at that teeming life in and above the great pools of salt water which cover so much of the earth's surface. To complete the picture, we must now consider the multitudinous pageant of life and color produced by the dry ground of the earth itself, culminating, of course, in those children of men, for whom it was all made.

As with all God's gifts, we take all that we see on the earth very much for granted, having known it from earliest childhood. But if we could suddenly see it for the first time when we were grown up, as might happen to someone born blind, perhaps we would never afterward forget our first gasp of astonishment, to begin with at the wonderful thing which the act of seeing is in itself, and then at the ever-changing patterns of color with which the earth is clothed, for, after all, everything might so easily have been the same color. Against the restful background of green there can surely be no color that has not been drawn out by the sun from some tiny seed moldering in the darkness in a handful of brown earth. Our Lord told the inhabitants of Galilee to look at the lily of the field—the scarlet anemone of the Palestinian hillsides—"for not even Solomon in all his glory was arrayed as one of these". For the Israelites the royal color was scarlet, such as Solomon would have worn, but for us, whose royal color is gold, the lesson comes home just as overwhelmingly if we gaze into the purest gold of a single buttercup among the myriads in the fields or at one of those countless dandelions, each one of which is like a reflection of the sun and would make any royal crown look dim.

In England the pageant of color seems to follow an ordered progress. As soon as the snows of winter have given place to the aptly-named snowdrops, which are like the flower-world's first gay mimics of the conquered snow, every color seems to come in its right turn to steal the pride of place in the picture. While the banks of snowlike blossom, tinged gradually with deepening pinks, still linger in the branches of the fruit trees, on the ground below the first cold white of the snowdrops and the anemones gives place, first to the pale primroses, then to the brighter yellow of the daffodils and finally to the dazzling gold of the buttercups and dandelions. And while out in the sunlight these myriads of little suns reflect the very image of that burning orb in the sky whose warmth has drawn them out of the earth; in the shade the blue of the sky itself is reflected in the carpets of bluebells. And finally, as the sun grows in heat, reds and purples begin to prevail, culminating in the fiery red of the poppies in the August corn and the mile upon mile of purple heather.

But, besides the colors of the flowers—made by God only for our delight, for the buttercup itself cannot see the gold with which its cup is burnished—there is another lesson which we may surely draw from the flowers, from the way in which they grow. All that is required from each plant, from the first stirring of life in the seed within the dark soil, is that it reach out toward the sun, whose warmth it feels, and it is simply by that striving to reach the warmth of the sun that, all unknown to itself, it takes on its lovely shape and color. So, too, it is with us. The more we try to live in the consciousness of the presence of God's burning love and to look only to him, as the flowers do to the sun, the more the warmth of his love will expand and transform our souls. And that brings us to the place of man himself in this visible world.

"And God created man to his own image: to the image of God he created him. Male and female he created them. And God blessed them, saying: Increase and multiply and fill the earth and subdue it, and rule over the fishes of the sea and the birds of the air and all living creatures that move upon the earth".

Wonderful as the visible world is, from the mightiest nebula blazing in the sky to the tiny blue butterfly sunning itself on a stone, it would all have been quite pointless if it had stopped short before the creation of man. Not only is it all doomed to extinction as the great lights are extinguished, but, even while it lasts, it is quite passive and unconscious in its obedience to the laws and instincts implanted in it. The buttercup does not know what it is doing when it draws out of a handful of brown earth that purest gold which makes even the crown of Solomon look dim. Nor does the month-old storm petrel know that floating on the surface of the ocean a thousand miles away there will be enough food to keep the warmth in its tiny body during all the long winter months.

To answer the riddle of this mysterious Treasure Island, spinning unconsciously in the midst of the great balls of fire, we need, like Robinson Crusoe on another island, to find the footprint of Man Friday in the sand. With his reason which is able to think about these things and with his capacity for love which is able to feel gratitude to the Creator who has made them for him, man is the answer to the question of why God made the visible world. Even with man, with his origin in the slime of the earth, the process is only a gradual one. In the natural order a child, when he is very young, takes his own existence for granted, as he does the warmth and food and comforting which answer his every cry. But very soon he begins to understand something of the love with which he is surrounded, above all by the love of his mother, and, in proportion as he understands, he begins to give back love for love. And love, of its nature, cannot be forced. It is a child's spontaneous throwing of his arms round his mother's neck that means so much to her, or the giving of a gift, however small, when she knows that it really costs the child something to part with it.

From God's point of view we must always seem like tiny children, however grown up we think we are, and the whole of this earth is really only like a warm and gaily-colored nursery, with lovely bright lights fastened in the ceiling, and stocked with far more food and toys than we could possibly need, if only we ourselves were not so destructive. At first, we take it all for granted, ourselves included, but as we grow older we begin to realize that it was somebody else who made us and who gave us all these lovely things. Even so, we find ourselves quite free. We can, if we like, ignore God, not bothering to remember whether he exists or not or why he made us, but concentrating on getting as many as possible of the good things he has given us which we can touch and see and taste. Or else, like a more normal child, we can give him a smile from time to time as he watches us playing with the toys he has given us, or even leave them sometimes just to come and be with him because we love him.

But however often we think of him and however much we love him, our love for him can never approach his love for us. We know from the inspired Scripture that a mother's love for her child is the least misleading simile we can use when we try to picture the nature of God—God, whose very essence is infinite love. "Can a mother forget her infant?... and even if she should forget, yet will I not forget thee". "As one whom the mother caresseth, so will I comfort thee". Anyone who has seen a mother bending over her baby's cot and trying to coax from him a smile of recognition has seen the nearest earthly likeness to the Divine Love.

And that freedom of ours—to ignore him, to give him an occasional grudging smile or, like Mary, to want to spend all our lives at his feet in complete surrender to his love—is our most stupendous privilege, given to us alone of all the visible creatures that God has made. And it is also a tremendous personal responsibility resting on each one of us, for each one of us is completely unique in the history of the world and like a separate creation. We, and we only, can give God the love of our particular heart. And in the whole eternity for which each one of us has been irrevocably created there is only this one brief period of our earthbound life during which God is watching to catch those fleeting little looks of love which he knows cost us an effort but which represent our real free spontaneous love.

While we are here on the earth, and because of our origin "out of the slime of the earth", he does not expect our love and homage to have the purity of the angels' or to be as ceaseless as theirs, but because of the Spirit which he breathed into us "to his own image and likeness", it really is the first stanza of the song of the angels in the presence of the Beatific Vision which we are beginning to learn. It is as though the spirit of some bright and glorious butterfly, created to soar into the sunshine and to live only on honey sipped from choicest flowers, were already astir in the creeping earthbound form of the caterpillar. And the nearer we draw to the time of our transformation, the more—however happy we may have been on earth—that restlessness should be growing inside us and that longing to see his face. For, as Saint Augustine once wrote: "Thou hast made us for thyself, O God, and our heart can never rest until it rests in thee".

That homesickness for God's infinite love and beauty, implanted in the human soul, gives man the supreme privilege of making articulate the unconscious worship of the other creatures. The other creatures do indeed praise God unconsciously by obeying the laws and instincts which he has implanted in them—we have but to think of the blind flowers reaching up to the sun whose warmth they feel, of the dawn chorus of the birds in springtime, their small bodies vibrating with music as they greet the return of the same life-giving warmth, or of the stars shining forth with cheerfulness to him who made them. But their dumb homage cannot, of course, compare in God's sight with the conscious and heartfelt love with which seven times in the day and in the silent watches of the night choirs of men and women make it the chief task of their brief sojourn on the earth to adore and bless with song the Creator of it all. His love is holding every tiny sparrow and storm petrel in existence and is so much greater for us that he has told us himself that the very hairs of our head are numbered by him.

DOM JULIAN STONOR, O.S.B.

LENTEN SERMONS

St. MARY'S, LIVERPOOL

1956

"THE LAMB OF GOD"

(1) CREATION, FALL, ABEL, MELCHISEDECH, ABRAHAM

(2) MOSES, "OUT OF EGYPT HAVE I CALLED MY SON"

(3) DAVID, TEMPLE, DISPERSAL, BETHLEHEM

(4) EPIPHANY, GALILEE, FINDING, BAPTISM

(5) 5,000, LAST SUPPER, CALVARY, EMMAUS, HEAVEN

(I)

BEHOLD THE LAMB OF GOD

The two previous preachers have spoken to you about the theory of God's Redemption. I want to speak to you about that Redemption in practice—what God has actually done.

The first words of the Bible are: "In the beginning God created heaven and earth. The world was waste and empty, and darkness covered it. And the Spirit of God brooded over it".

—There we have the first mention of God's loving care, which will so often be repeated.

Then, very briefly, the setting is described: the creation of the three materials out of which our whole universe is made:

1. Light (because the whole universe is really nothing but a vast array of burning lights).
2. The Two Firmaments: the upper firmament of space, which separates the various lights; and the more condensed lower firmament of air and water, which surrounds our earth and circles round with it, enabling us to live and breathe.
3. The Earth Itself: the dry ground, with its minerals and vegetation.

Then, equally briefly, the three armies of moving things are described, which are made out of these materials:

1. The vast array of individual lights or stars which move on their courses in the depths of space.
2. The myriads of creatures which live in the waters, and those which have developed wings to fly in the air.
3. And, finally, the animals who have developed upon the dry ground and live upon what it provides.

All these creatures were made by God for the service of man, who was to be the special object of his love, almost a reflection of it. "Let us make man to our own image and likeness". Now, "God is Love"—the infinite love uniting the Father and the Son, in the Holy Spirit. Therefore, man is love, made to the image of this divine love.

Now, we all know that love must give itself absolutely freely. If it is forced in any way, it isn't love. That is what makes it so

207

precious, and why a mother spends so many hours bending over her baby trying to coax it to give her a smile.

Therefore, when God made man to his own image and likeness, a creature that was able to love him, he had to leave him absolutely free. Even though man owed his very existence to God, he could give God his love, or he could withhold it. And, as we know, he chose to withhold it. When the creation of the setting was described, we were told again and again: "God saw that it was good", and, finally, "God saw all things that He had made, and they were very good". No words could emphasize more clearly the coming tragedy, when men were going to bring evil into the world.

At this point Moses has inserted into the Book of Genesis a divinely inspired tradition concerning the fall of man's first parents, which is many centuries earlier than the rest of the book. Its whole language is quite different, even the word for "God"; everything about it reflects those earliest days of the human race in the hot desert lands of Babylonia.

We are told of a shady oasis in the desert—"Paradise" is the ancient Persian word for "oasis" and "Eden" for a "desert": of how God formed the first man "out of the slime of the earth" and "breathed into him the breath of life", so that he became "a living soul"; and of how God placed him in this oasis in the desert, "to dress it and tend it".

Then comes the famous story of the temptation. The very names seem to show how the whole of human history was contained in that first refusal of man to give to his Creator the love for which he had asked. For the name "Adam" simply means "man", and the word used for "fruit" is the word for "evil", as is still the case with the Saxon word "apple" or its Latin equivalent "malus".

The tempter promised Adam and Eve that if they disobeyed God's command and ate this evil fruit, they would be as gods and their own judges of good and evil. The early men, when they handed down that inspired story to us, did not know of the fallen angels. But it is easy for us to see who that tempter was. For when Satan, whose very existence at each moment depended like ours, on God's love, refused to give to his Creator the love for which he had been created, he was put to shame by the archangel Michael, whose very name—"Mich-a-el" means "Who can be the equal of God?"

And we know that for the duration of this world Satan is allowed by God to use his freedom in trying to induce men to join his own pathetic rebellion. We have only to think of that sorry procession in our own days—Mussolini, Hitler, Stalin, and all the others—who claimed to be equal to God, and to have the power to decide for themselves, and for others, what is good and what is evil.

And the ironical thing is that God's response to that first rebellion of his human creatures was, from the very beginning, to bring it about that they should become the real equals of his only Son. For, by becoming one of us, and by making amends to his Father as one of us, God the Son was to win for us everything that is his. He has put himself between God the Father and us, so that the Father sees, not us and our sins, but his own Son pleading from the cross. And when we go to heaven, we will be loved by God the Father, and love him back, just as the Son himself.

And so we come to the gradual unfolding to men of this plan of God's, and we meet the touching image of the innocent lamb.

When we look back to the beginnings of our human history, as far back as our eyes can see, the same inspired tradition which told us of the fall of Adam and Eve told us one other story: how Cain murdered his brother, Abel, "because his own works were evil and his brother's just".

Abel, the shepherd, whose name in ancient Persian means "my son", was to be the first of many prophetic foreshadowings of God the Son, the coming Redeemer. And, all down the ages, men would remember his poured-out blood pleading to God from the earth, mingled with the blood of the lamb which he had just offered to God.

The next great prophetic figure is Abraham. Leaving the pagan people of Babylonia, who had lost the true knowledge of God, he came to Palestine to become the father of a people with whom God would renew that covenant of love, which he had made with the family of Noe [Noah] after the flood.

And now the very spot will be marked out—two thousand years in advance—where the actual Redemption will take place.

Already for many years there had stood on the hilltop of Moriah a little fortified town named Salem—afterward to be called Jeru-Salem, "Holy Salem". From Salem there now came forth, to meet and bless Abraham, its ruler Melchisedech ("the

King of Justice", his name means)—"for he was a priest of the
most high God".

The sacrifice which he offered was, not a lamb, but bread and
wine, and that this sacrifice of his in bread and wine was something even more solemn than the myriads of lambs which would
be offered on this spot in the next two thousand years was to
be a constant part of Jewish belief. A thousand years later, King
David would write that the coming Redeemer would be "a priest
forever, according to the order of Melchisedech". And a thousand
years later still, on that very spot the promised Redeemer, the true
King of Justice, would found his kingdom and give to men the
new world-wide, ceaseless, sacrifice of his own Body and Blood
under the form of bread and wine.

And even the terrible death which he then went out to undergo
had been foretold to us two thousand years before. For, some ten
years after Abraham's meeting with Melchisedech an even more
moving event took place.

Once again, the very names of the actors emphasize the meaning,
for "Abraham" means literally "the love of a father", and the name
of his son, "Isaac", means "May God be appeased". God said to
him: "Take thy only-begotten son, Isaac, whom thou lovest, and
go into the land of vision, and there thou shalt offer him for a
holocaust upon the hill which I shall show thee".

Now, "the land of vision" is "Moriah" in Hebrew, the very hill
on which Salem, Jerusalem, stands. It means literally "the place
where God sees you", and it almost certainly received that name
from Abraham himself because of what was now to happen there,
for God was to show him that he was watching him all the time.

As we watch Abraham's only-begotten son, whom he loved—that
son who bore the prophetic name "May God be appeased"—climbing Mount Moriah with his father—whose very name, we remember, meant "the love of a father"—and carrying the wood on which
he was to be sacrificed on the summit—on Calvary, we, of course,
see that other cross-laden figure, God's only-begotten Son, who was
one day to climb that same hill. And, to bring home to ourselves
the full realization of what God seemed to be asking of Abraham
during the moments when he actually held the sword in his hand
with which to slay his son whom he loved so much, we have only
to think of Our Lady as she sat on that same spot with the dead

body of her Son in her arms, with its gaping wound in the heart.

Abraham was spared that final agony. And, in the ram, caught in the briars, which he was allowed to substitute for his son, and in the myriads of year-old rams which were afterward to be offered on that hill, we are, of course, meant to see already the true Lamb, who on the hilltop would substitute himself for us all and win for us, not only God's forgiveness, but a love which we will understand only in heaven.

Some such memories as these should be in our minds when, immediately after the Consecration of every Mass, we beg God the Father to "Deign to look down on our sacrifice, as thou didst deign to accept the offering of thy just son, Abel, and the sacrifice of our father, Abraham, and that which thy great priest Melchisedech, offered to thee".

(2)

"OUT OF EGYPT I HAVE CALLED MY SON"

That call, of God to man, to leave the material comforts, and discomforts, of Egypt and come to him, in trust and faith, to a home which we have not yet seen, is a call that has been made to each single one of us, whether we like it or not. It is not just something which happened to the children of Israel, but, like so many things which happened to them, it was a foreshadowing, in vivid picture language, of God's plan for each one of us. Our answer to that call is our part in the plan of the Redemption.

We have to leave, of our own free will, the home which we have spoilt by introducing evil, and journey to a new home, where we can start again and where the memory of the rebellion will have been washed away. But we are meant to begin in the Egypt of this earth, just as we are meant to end up in heaven. It is just as much God's plan for us as it is for a caterpillar to begin its life crawling about on its tummy eating cabbage leaves and to end as a gorgeous butterfly which can fly wherever it wants and live on honey.

We saw yesterday how the whole of this material universe was created for man. It is the nursery world, in which we begin our life—that life which is never going to end. And just as a small child in a nursery takes his own existence for granted, as he does the warmth and food and playthings which surround him, so we take ourselves and all that God has given us for granted at first—and some people do so all their lives on this earth.

The night sky blazing with stars no longer means anything to us in this cloudy corner of the world with our artificial lights to keep us indoors. Those great lights in the sky might just as well have already burned themselves out, though we can at least imagine how they must have impressed our earliest forefathers, who spent their long nights out on the sands of eastern deserts.

But, before passing on to the subject of this morning's talk, I would like to give you just one tiny example of what I meant when I said that everything in this material world was made for us. Our Lord once pointed out the scarlet anemone, which covers the hillsides of Galilee in the spring, and told his hearers to consider it, how not even Solomon in all the glory of his royal scarlet could compare with it. But why was it there at all? For us, who associate gold, rather than scarlet, with royalty, the commonest flower of early summer is, appropriately, the buttercup, and we only have to look into one of those golden cups among the myriads in the field to realize that it would make the gold of any royal crown look dim. But why are they there?

My point is that the buttercup itself cannot see the gold with which its cup is burnished—it can only reach out blindly and unconsciously toward the warmth of the sun. Its color, like the scarlet of the anemone, like the taste of the strawberry, or like the scent of the rose, is only to please us.

But, however beautifully a children's nursery is decorated, and however well stocked it is with toys, it is only a temporary arrangement. Before very long, the child will grow up, and eventually will go out into the world to find a home of his own. And so it is with this world. We are in it for only a very, very, short time, compared with eternity. Our real home is to be in heaven. And because God is infinite love, and knows what he has prepared for us, he calls us relentlessly to make that the object of our longings.

I want to take now that famous journey of the children of Israel from Egypt to the Promised Land; as I said, the whole thing is—in vivid picture language, such as we use to teach small children to read—a prophecy of the journey each one of us has to make from the familiar Egypt of the earth to our promised home in heaven. And, as you would see repeatedly if you read the

whole story, they were just as reluctant to leave Egypt, or even
the desert, for Jerusalem and the Promised Land as most men are
to leave this earth, which they know, for the heavenly Jerusalem
which is our promised home.

The chief human actor in the story is Moses, another great
prophetical figure of Christ like the ones we considered yesterday.
From the death sentence, decreed by Pharaoh against all male
infants of the Hebrews, he, the future redeemer of his people
had been the only child saved, just as the true Redeemer was
to be the only child saved from the massacre of the infants by
King Herod. He had been brought up at the royal court in all the
wisdom and learning of the Egyptians—(the great books of laws
which he drew up for the Israelites in the desert many years later
show us something of what that education was)—until, as Saint
Paul puts it: "By faith Moses, when he was grown up, denied
himself to be the son of Pharaoh's daughter, rather choosing to
be afflicted with the People of God". And because he had left the
glory of the Egyptian court and identified himself with those
poor outcast slaves, he was even more truly a prophetic image of
Divine Pity itself, the Son of God, who was to leave the glory of
the heavenly courts and identify himself with the poor outcast
children of man. And, like Christ, his prayer for those rebellious,
ungrateful, children would always be: "Father, forgive them, for
they know not what they do".

When the time came for Moses to carry out that prophetic
redemption of the children of Israel from Egypt, we meet once
more the image of the lamb. From now, until the coming of the
true Lamb a thousand years later, it will occupy the center of the
stage. For their last supper on the eve of the great day, each family was to take a lamb that had been sacrificed to God, to smear
some of its blood on the wood of their doorposts (for where that
blood was, no harm could come to them), and then to eat its flesh,
whole and entire—a command which would only become fully
clear at that paschal supper when the true Lamb himself would
say: "Take you all, and eat; for this is my body" and "This is my
blood, which will be poured out for you".

Meanwhile, for over a thousand years, that image of a lamb,
whose blood was poured out for them and whose flesh they were
to eat, would remain the center of their lives. Day by day, whether

they were in the desert or whether, after they had reached Jeru-salem, they were in the Temple, every morning and evening and whenever a man wanted to atone for some sin, a lamb was led to the entrance of the tabernacle; there, the priest laid his hands on its head—to symbolize man's identifying himself with it—and, after it had been sacrificed, its blood would be sprinkled on the altar and toward the veil which symbolized the inaccessible throne of God—the poured-out blood, as it were, showing itself to God, as the blood of Abel had done, and pleading for his pity and forgiveness.

And, every year, when the night on which they had been saved from Egypt came round, the ritual of the blood-stained wood was repeated in every home, and at the supper the children had to ask their parents: "Why is this night different from all the other nights of the year?"—to make sure that the story would never be forgotten.

Immediately after that first paschal supper the children of Israel set out on their journey to the Promised Land. And, underlying all that was to happen to them, was this great prophecy of the future Redemption of all mankind. Redeemed by the blood of the lamb and having passed through the baptismal waters of the Red Sea, they would journey through a land where they could not see God, but would be fed each morning on "bread from heaven". After the fiftieth day ("Pentecost" in Greek), guided by the Holy Spirit in the midst of them, symbolized by the column of incense smoke by day and the glow of the fire by night rising from the golden altar in the Holy Place, they would finally reach the Promised Land, where they would be God's people, and God, in the midst of them, would be their God.

But that prophetical significance was largely for us. For them God's great longing was to make them see that they could trust him, not only to provide them with the promised home, but to provide for their needs on the way—to prove to them by repeated signs, the reality of his providence—the same message which was to take up so large a part of Our Lord's teaching.

I will give you two examples:

Take, first, the crossing of the Red Sea. Bible story books often picture for us something like the Mersey, with water parting to form two high walls, and the Israelites marching triumphantly down the middle. Actually, before the cutting of the Suez Canal (not very many years ago) there were several caravan routes, by which they could have entered Sinai dry-shod. And where they did cross, a few miles south of the Bitter Lakes, there was a shallow ford made by a sand bar, which in the hot summer was often left high and dry, but in the spring would be covered by a very shallow water.

Moses's own account tells us that, after a hot east wind from the Sinai desert had blown all the previous night (perhaps carrying tons of fresh sand with it as it often does), this sand bar was left so dry that the waters became divided and they were able to march across dry-shod, while the expanses of water on either side were like protecting shields or walls against a flank attack by the Egyptians. But the thousands of feet would have churned up the sand, and when, on the following day, a strong south wind brought back the waters, the heavy Egyptian two-horsed chariots sank in the sand and water. It was the timing of it all which made it a sign and proved God's providence.

Then, when they found themselves in the desert country on the other side, there was a panic about food, "And the children of Israel said: Would to God we had died by the hand of the Lord in the land of Egypt, when we sat over the flesh-pots and ate bread to the full. Why have you brought us into this desert that you might destroy all the multitude with famine? And the Lord said to Moses, Behold, I will rain bread from heaven for you. Let the people go forth and gather what is sufficient for every day. And when the dew fell in the night, the manna also fell with it. And the people went about and gathered it, and ground it in a mill or beat it in a mortar, and then boiled it in a pot and made cakes thereof".

What the Arabs still call "manna" are little yellowish-brown balls of sugar, white when they are crushed, which are let fall during the night by insects feeding on the leaves of the tamarisk trees. They must be gathered early in the morning before the ants devour them. The present yield of the Sinai desert is only six hundredweight, but countless tamarisk trees have been destroyed by the Arabs for firewood.

And so one could go on, with all the famous signs that God wrought for them—the fresh meat, the water, the crossing of the River Jordan, the collapse of the walls of Jericho, and so on. Always there is a perfectly natural explanation, but always too there is the wonderful timing of it, to prove to them that God was watching over them, that he had seen their needs in advance—for that is what the word "providence" means.

It is this comforting assurance that Our Lord wanted us to draw, not only from signs and wonders, but, as I explained at the beginning, from everything which he has put into this world for us—"Your Father knoweth that you have need of all these things".

(3)

"BEHOLD THE LAMB OF GOD WHO TAKETH AWAY THE SINS OF THE WORLD"

When the long journey of which I spoke yesterday, was at last over, there followed three centuries in the history of the Redemption, during which no great figure reflected the love and pity of the coming Redeemer as Abraham and Moses had done. But then there arose a third such figure—the shepherd-king David, whose name means "the beloved son".

The exploits of his early years against the lions and against the Philistines, and his sins too, are very like those of Samson a hundred years before. But the tragedy of Samson—the ever-increasing self-confidence and carelessness in the battle between the spirit and the flesh, until, finally, he allowed himself to lose the unshorn locks of the Nazarite, the outward sign that God had laid his hand upon that head in consecration—does not move us as does the real remorse and renewed trust that followed hard on King David's falls. No one could have shown greater ingratitude than David's son, Absolom; yet never was the love of any father for a prodigal son expressed more sadly than in that cry which still moves us after three thousand years: "O my son, Absolom; O Absolom, my son. Would to God that I might have died for thee; O, Absolom—my son, my son".

With King David the altar-hill of Jerusalem comes into the story again. It was on the very spot on the hill known as "Moriah", where Abraham had been allowed to sacrifice the ram as a substitute for his son, Isaac, that now God stopped the plague at King David's prayer of repentance, and on that actual spot his son, Solomon, was commanded to build the great temple for the sacrifice of the lambs—the one and only spot on the whole surface of the earth where they were to be offered.

Every morning, when the priest on the roof of the Temple saw the first light of the new day glimmering over the Mount of Olives, the shrill notes of silver trumpets announced to the inhabitants of Jerusalem that the victim was being led to the altar. Day by day, century after century, it would go on and, as sins against the letter of the Law became multiplied by the priests, the never-ending stream of private sin-offerings grew ever greater—a ceaseless stream of blood running down over the rock of Mount Moriah.

With only one church for the whole world in which sacrifices could be offered, there was bound to be congestion. And when gifts were demanded for every petty trespass against the letter of the Law, the Temple vaults became stacked with incredible quantities of gold and meat and corn, and the great court of the Gentiles was filled from end to end with the cattle-market and the sheep-market and those stalls of the money-changers which Our Lord was to overthrow. Only Levitically-perfect lambs could be offered—obviously one would not offer to God a lamb that was deformed—and, in practice, only a lamb which had been bought from the priests themselves was certain to pass the scrutiny. What a far cry this was from the touching gesture of Abel, offering back to God the firstling of his flock in the springtime of the world!

"To what purpose do you offer me the multitude of your victims? saith the LORD.... I desire not holocausts of rams ... and the blood of lambs.... For all the beasts of the woods are mine and the cattle on the hills.... Offer to God the sacrifice of praise, and call upon me in the day of trouble".

Those centuries, during which the Temple stood on Mount Sion [Zion] and the chosen people dwelt with God in the Promised Land, were to be one more sad commentary on the use which men make of their freedom. Just before they entered it, Moses had reminded them once more how "in the wilderness, as thou hast seen, the LORD thy God hath carried thee as a man is wont to carry his little son". But now, like their first parents when they were placed in Paradise, they were to disobey and to make themselves their own judges of good and evil. God had commanded them through Moses to destroy utterly the debased and corrupted inhabitants of the land, who sacrificed their own babies to Moloch and Baal, and there in a cleansed land his people would dwell secure. And then:

"As the shepherd visiteth his flock in the day when he shall be in the midst of his sheep, so will I visit my sheep. I will seek that which was lost and bind up that which was broken, and I will bring them to their own land. I will feed them in the most fruitful pastures, and their pastures shall be the high mountains of Israel; there they shall rest on the green grass".

He had kept his promise, but they would not keep theirs. Yet, however black their ingratitude, he still took advantage of every little tentative groping toward him in their days of trouble to tell them again and again, that he would never forget them, however often they forgot him.

"And Israel said: The LORD has forgotten me and the LORD has forsaken me. Can a mother forget her own child? And even if she should forget, yet will I not forget thee. For a small moment have I hidden my face from thee for a little while, but with everlasting pity will I gather thee. O poor little one, tossed with tempests, without all comfort ... thou shalt not fear. As one whom the mother caresseth, so will I comfort you. I will draw thee with bonds of love, because I am God, and not man, the Holy One in the midst of thee. Destruction is thine own, O Israel; thy help is only in me".

But, in spite of God's continual pleading with them through his prophets, it was to other gods that they turned—gods who demanded the murder of children, gods who could not deliver them.

"Oh, all ye, who pass by the way, attend and see if there be any sorrow like unto my sorrow. My sorrow is above sorrow, my heart mourneth within me ... for the affliction of the daughter of my people ... I said: Return to me; and she did not return. Return, you rebellious children, and I will heal your rebellions. But they made their faces harder than the rock and refused to return".

But in the very destruction and humiliation which they brought upon themselves, they were enabling God to fulfil his plan of love and forgiveness, of which the great prophets were already beginning to dream. "He has therefore scattered you among the Gentiles who know him not, that you may declare his wonderful works and make them know that there is no other God beside him". It was not for the Jews alone that the true Lamb was soon to come and die, but for all the peoples of the human race.

In their exile, scattered throughout the whole inhabited world, the Jews turned to their God and to his chosen city, Jerusalem, with an intensity of homesick longing, which drew with it thousands of Gentile souls, weary of the worn-out paganism of the East and of Greece and Rome. "By the waters of Babylon we sat down, and wept, when we remembered Sion.... And they that had led us into captivity said: Sing ye to us a hymn of the songs of Sion".

Since even greater crowds of Gentiles flocked each year to Jerusalem for the great sacrifice of the paschal lambs than stayed on for the feast of Pentecost seven weeks later, we may feel sure that all those "Parthians and Medes and Elamites and inhabitants of Mesopotamia and Cappadocia, Pontus and Asia, Phrygia and Pamphylia, Egypt and the parts of Lybia about Cyrene and strangers of Rome, Cretes also and Arabians" who were there at Pentecost, seven weeks after Our Lord's death, were in the city too when, just outside its main gate, the Lamb of God was taking away the sins of the whole world.

For, at last, the longed-for day had come: "the desire of the ever-lasting hills".

As it had been for a thousand years, Bethlehem had, that day, been filled with the bleating of lambs. For century after century, it had always been in the fields round this little township of shepherds, six miles from Jerusalem, that the thousands of year-old lambs were folded, while they waited their turn to be led to the altar in the Temple.

King David had been a shepherd of Bethlehem, like his father and brothers before him. And so it had been to the village of the shepherds that Joseph and Mary came, when, in the fullness of time, the true Lamb of God was to be born.

It would not have been in a stable for horses and cows, but in a shelter for sheep, that on Christmas night the shepherds found him lying in the hay in a manger. And, during those first months, the sound that must have been most often in his ears must have been the bleating of all those thousands of other sacrificial lambs in the fields outside, which, all unconsciously represented him alone. All through his life, that sound was never to be very far away.

Some of the very lambs over which the shepherds had been watching on the night of his birth would be penned, rather frightened, in the Temple court on the morning when his mother came to offer him to God. And what a touching ceremony it was—that Jewish offering of a first-born to God. By refusing to make a return of love to its Creator, the only reason for which it had been made, the human race had in theory forfeited its right to go on existing; so the first-born son was handed back to God to be slain. But when the mother then quickly offered a lamb to the priest, her child was returned to her with a blessing, and the lamb was slain instead.

Away from their home, Joseph and Mary were unable to afford a lamb, and were allowed to offer two turtle-doves instead. But in any case no other lamb could ever be substituted for this child; when she received him back from the arms of the priest, his mother was to hear, not a blessing, but that sad warning: "Thy own soul a sword shall pierce". And it would only be a few months before she would feel the first stab of that sword.

(4)
"SEND FORTH, O LORD, THE LAMB, THE RULER OF THE EARTH"

As we have seen, the human race began in the hot, dry, land of Babylonia, and it is there that all the history recorded in the Bible took place until the departure of Abraham. In the crystal clear air of Mesopotamia the desert sky each night becomes a shimmering, scintillating, mass of stars, so awe-inspiring and so seemingly endowed with life and movement that the Babylonians had begun to worship them as beings far more wonderful and powerful than themselves. In the great church at Ur, the city which Abraham left, we can still read a lovely prayer to the "Father, long-suffering and full of forgiveness, whose hand upholds the life of mankind"; but the person to whom that prayer was addressed they had begun to identify with the moon.

But, even though Abraham left Babylonia forever, to found a race who would hand down the true picture of God until from one of their own daughters, the Son of God would take our human flesh, there would still be many links with the land of their first ancestors. Abraham's only son, Isaac, and Isaac's son, Jacob, would both journey to Babylonia to choose their brides. And in the sixth century before the coming of Christ the whole Jewish people was deported to Babylonia, including the great prophets, Ezekiel and Daniel, who became the head of the great Babylonian college of priests and wise men. And by the time of Our Lord many Baby-lonians were journeying to Palestine each year for the great feasts.

But what seems so particularly true to the whole pattern of God's merciful providence is that he should have used the very errors into which they had fallen, through their being fascinated by the glory of the stars, to bring them, before anyone else except the Bethlehem shepherds, to pay their homage to the divine child, who was just as truly a child of their race as he was of the Jews.

It has now been established that Our Lord was born in BC 8 (that was the year of the census under Cyrinus, and King Herod the persecutor died in BC 4). Now, in the autumn of BC 7 and again in the spring of BC 6, two events occurred in the sky which had not happened for sixteen centuries and were not due to occur again until the years 1603 and 1604, when they were witnessed and described by the great German astronomer, Kepler. One day in the autumn there was what is known as a conjunction of the planets, Jupiter and Saturn, and, one day in the following spring a conjunction of three planets, Jupiter, Saturn, and Mars. It means that, as viewed from this earth, they would on these two days, so to speak, catch one another up; the result, as described by Kepler, was what appeared to be one large heavenly body of such brightness that it was visible even at midday.

When this phenomenon first appeared in the autumn sky of BC 7, we can imagine how those Babylonian priests or magi would have become convinced, however mistakenly, that it portended some very great event on earth. And the universal expectation of the Jewish Messiah, the time of whose coming had been calculated by Daniel in their own Babylon, would soon convince them that his birth must be that great event.

That their embassy the following spring to Jerusalem, where they would expect the future King of the Jews to be born, was far more than just the three figures on camels, whom we have grown accustomed to imagining because of the three gifts, seems clear from the fact that the whole city was thrown into an uproar and a special meeting of the Sanhedrin had to be summoned by King Herod. After all, pilgrims from the East poured into Jerusalem every day and no one would have noticed just three Persian priests, whatever stories they had to tell about a star.

Later that evening, as the embassy proceeded on its way to the village of Bethlehem, the second conjunction of the three planets suddenly occurred in the southern sky right in front of them, and seemed, as a star does, to move before them as they rode; when they had actually paid their homage, they could point to this great star above and to the child below and show, as the account preserved in the gospels says they did, their "exceeding great joy".

I have told this story is some detail because I always think that it is meant to hold a far higher place in the story of our Redemption than is usually given to it. Among the feasts of the Church the Epiphany has always ranked next after Easter and Pentecost. It is the feast of the first public appearance of Our Lord to the world he had come to save. And the timing of it all—the bringing of the Magi on to that Bethlehem road on just the one evening when that phenomenon in the sky would re-appear—makes it just as wonderful an example of God's all-seeing providence as anything that happened to the children of Israel on their journey from Egypt to the Promised Land. And even the gold and spices offered in homage by the Magi were a part of that providence—to provide for the needs of the Holy Family on their journey to Egypt, during their two year stay there, and for their journey back from Egypt to the Promised Land.

Of its brief year of life a paschal lamb, destined for sacrifice, would spend by far the greater part on the hillsides of Galilee, in peace and security beside its mother; only in its last weeks going to those grim folds in Bethlehem and Bethany to await its death in Jerusalem. And so, in that too, the true Lamb would conform to the pattern. On his return from Egypt, he would not go back to Bethlehem, but would spend the next thirty of the thirty-three years remaining to him dwelling, unknown to all except his mother, in a hillside village in Galilee.

Only one incident has come down to us, and that too can only be explained in terms of the lamb. Every year, he went with his mother and foster-father to Jerusalem for the great paschal sacrifice of the lambs. Now, when a boy entered on his thirteenth year, he became "a son of the Law"—for the first time it became his own responsibility to observe it—and since the chief object of the Law is that our love and obedience to God should come first, we can understand how Our Lord wanted his first action as "a son of the Law" to be the beginning of the work which his Father has sent him to do. "How is it that you sought me? Did you not know that I must be about my Father's business?"

He could easily have told his parents beforehand, and saved them those three days of anxiety. Why was it that he, whose love and obedience to his parents just as much as to God was absolutely perfect, deliberately allowed them to lose him? The answer is, surely, in the nature of the work his Father had given him to do.

During the eight days after the Pasch the rabbis gave instructions in the Temple court to the throngs of pilgrims. And when he began to answer the questions of the rabbis as to the true meaning of the great paschal sacrifice, his mother at least would have understood at once that he was to be the true Lamb of God. He knew that the sword would there and then have pierced her heart and that for the next twenty-five years she would never have known real happiness. He had to put his Father's will first, but when, in considering the pain it would inevitably cause his mother, he was faced with the choice of causing her twenty-five years of that haunting knowledge or three days of anxiety with a happy ending, how could he hesitate?

The last act of the drama would open on a February day twenty-five years later. The first scene was deep in the Jordan valley opposite Jericho, where, more than a thousand years before, on the feast of the paschal lamb, the children of Israel had crossed the providentially dried-up river and entered the Promised Land. And this section of the Jordan valley was the one on which the aged Moses had gazed down from Mount Nebo, the highest point of its eastern wall, when he gave his last blessing to the chosen people, and told them: "The LORD thy God will raise up to thee a Prophet, of thy nation and of thy brethren, like unto me. Him shalt thou hear". Those words would now be echoed by the voice of God himself.

That was the historical setting of the scene. And in the background, like an orchestral refrain, was the sound we have now come to expect, the bleating of thousands of lambs. But this bleating was more plaintive even than that of Bethlehem, for here, in this sheltered valley in February, it was the crying of new-born lambs, and lambs which were frightened.

For huge crowds of men were flocking into the valley from all sides. A prophet, the first for many centuries, was preaching that the kingdom of God was at hand. The word had gone round that it was Elias, returned to the earth, and so great were the crowds that gathered to hear him that even young fishermen from far-away Galilee were helping to marshal them.

Nearly six weeks previously, a young carpenter, also from Galilee, had presented himself to be baptized, and the sign had come for which John had been waiting. As Jesus had prayed, John "saw the Holy Spirit descending upon him in the likeness of a dove, and a voice came from heaven: Thou art my beloved Son; in thee I am well-pleased".

But then Jesus had disappeared again into the desert hills. Now, forty days later, "John saw Jesus coming to him, and he saith: Behold, the lamb of God: behold, him who taketh away the sins of the world... and, the next day, again John stood, and two of his disciples, and, beholding Jesus walking, he saith: Behold, the lamb of God". In the silence that would have fallen over them as they looked at the walking figure, they would hear again the frightened bleating of the new-born lambs in the hills, and that would be sufficient commentary on that terrible title.

(5)

"BUT THOU, O LORD, HAST SHOWN ME AND I HAVE KNOWN; THOU SHOWEDST ME THEIR DOINGS, AND I WAS AS A MEEK LAMB THAT IS CARRIED TO BE A VICTIM". "HE WAS OFFERED, BECAUSE IT WAS HIS OWN WILL, AND HE OPENED NOT HIS MOUTH. HE SHALL BE LED AS A SHEEP TO THE SLAUGHTER".

It was very hot in the low hills of Bethsaida on the north shore of the Lake of Galilee. It was a heat that was to be the prelude to a great storm that night. For nearly three days the huge crowds of excited, gesticulating men had had nothing to eat except what they had brought round the lake with them. But they had other things to think about besides food. At last, the leader promised them by Moses seemed to have arisen. During the last few months his fame had been sweeping through the lakeside villages, and more and more people were now becoming convinced that this man could command sufficient authority to head an insurrection, drive out the Romans, and restore the kingdom of David. "But some said: Doth the anointed one come out of Galilee? Doth not the Scripture say that the anointed one cometh of the seed of David and from Bethlehem, the town where David was?" The prophet Micheas [Micah] had spoken so clearly: "And thou, Bethlehem, art a little one among the thousands of Juda, but out of thee shall he come forth that is to be the ruler of Israel, and his going forth is from the beginning, from the days of eternity". And none of them knew that he had been born in Bethlehem.

When the hottest part of the afternoon was over, his chosen followers began forcing their way through the dense crowds, telling the men to form up in ranks of a hundred and making enquiries about the food supply, and hopes began to mount to fever pitch that the nationalist army was about to be enrolled. Eventually, as evening drew on, the rays of the westerly sun would have fallen upon serried ranks of veiled tribesmen, tier above tier, squatting on the grassy hillside, while the thousands of women and children remained in a huddled anxious crowd in the valley.

A hush would have fallen over this vast throng as the twelve disciples returned to where their leader stood. For some minutes they hid him from view. Then Peter, followed by the others, was seen approaching the leading man of the front rank. What his feelings were as he did so, with a small piece of barley cake in his hand and thousands of pairs of eyes riveted upon him, we can barely imagine. Moses must have felt much the same when, in front of the whole Jewish people, he approached the solid-looking rock wall with the rod in his hand.

An hour or two later, when all in the huge crowd had eaten their fill, the disciples again began forcing their way down the excited ranks, each collecting any pieces that were left over until all twelve baskets were full, and everywhere the words "manna" and "king" could be heard, as the word flew from mouth to mouth that this must be the new Moses, the promised Messiah.

By now it must have been nearly dark, and the wind was getting up. And, to their consternation, the disciples were told to return in the boat without their Master. With the darkness there came a full gale, and in the fourth watch of the night, the one just before the dawn, as the heavily-laden boat was driven helplessly and in pitch darkness among the drenching waves, suddenly there was an apparition. They could just see that a figure like that of their Master appeared to be moving past them in the teeth of the wind. Probably the icy fear gripped them that the disappointed crowd had slain their Master, as they had tried to do once before, and that this was his spirit on its way to the next life. But as they cried out in terror, they heard three words (in the Aramaic) above the storm: "Be of good heart, it is I. Be not afraid".

For a moment, Peter's impetuous courage returned, and he called out: "Lord, if it be thou, bid me to come to thee upon the waters". And the answer came back: "Come!" But when, a moment later, he found himself plunging in the icy cold water, his faith was only strong enough to cry out: "Lord, save me". At once Our Lord was beside him and helping him into the boat: and probably amusement and love were what lay behind his severe question: "O thou of little faith, why didst thou doubt?" as they would lie behind his threefold: "Simon Peter, lovest thou me?"

After his experiences in the last eighteen hours of what his Master could do with bread and with the laws that normally govern our bodies, can we wonder that Peter could not doubt when, later that morning, their Master was to ask them to believe the hardest of his sayings for our minds to grasp:

"I am the true Bread from heaven.... Except you eat the flesh of the Son of Man and drink his blood, you shall not have life in you".

The Pasch was very near now—that supreme day, to which all the history of the ages had been leading up, and to which all succeeding ages would look back. Soon he was waiting in Bethany. The world around him seemed determined to make him king. Already there had been carpets down in the streets and a long procession shouting: "Hosanna to the son of David, the King of Israel". And Peter had managed to procure two swords in preparation for the coronation on Friday.

On the Thursday he remained in Bethany all day—in prayer. That day the Temple was closed to all except the long queues of men, each leading a lamb, who had come to keep the Pasch in Jerusalem. And as each batch of lambs was slain, the penetrating notes of the silver trumpets would reach the hillside of Bethany where he was preparing for his own immolation on the morrow.

Then, when the sun had set and the full paschal moon risen, he set out with his apostles toward Jerusalem and his death. Never, of course, would the three stages of the paschal supper be so charged with meaning as that night. To the singing of the first

Hallel ("Blesssed art thou, O Eternal, who redeemeth Israel") the bitter "haroseth" sauce would be brought in—symbolic hitherto of the bitterness of the Egyptian slavery, but now of all the sins of the world—and the bitterest drop would be added when Judas dipped his morsel of bread into the sauce with Our Lord and asked, "is it I, Lord?" and then went out into the night.

But the traditional rite proceeded—for the last time before it would be "fulfilled" in the new kingdom that was being founded. The pathetic symbol of redemption—the lamb whose blood had been poured out at the altar that afternoon, was brought in, fastened to its cross-like spits of wood in such a way that not a bone of its body should be broken.

And then, finally, came the thanksgiving—the Eucharist, as the Greek-speaking Jews called it—when they reclined once more to partake of the fruits of the Promised Land. To symbolize their perfect unity as children of one father (hitherto Abraham, but henceforth God the Father himself) a single flat loaf of unleavened bread would be broken and divided between them all and each cup would be filled from a single great chalice of wine.

Only now would the rite be changed and the new sacrifice, foretold by Melchisedech on this very spot, be given to mankind. "Take ye, and eat: this is my body which will be broken for you". "Take ye, and drink: this is the chalice of my blood, of the new testament, which will be poured out for many unto the remission of sins". "This do ye in memory of me".

By the same time tomorrow evening, his body would be lying white and bloodless in the tomb, and the blood that had drained in agony from it would be soaking into the dust of Calvary and pleading for forgiveness for the whole world.

He need not have suffered anything—he could have just asked his Father to forgive us—"he was offered, because he himself willed it", because he wanted us to see the full extent of man's ingratitude and hatred and how, in spite of that, he only wanted us to be forgiven.

Writers and preachers often give us the most harrowing descriptions of Our Lord's physical sufferings as the most terrible there have ever been and thereby distract our attention from the true meaning of it all. Physical pain is not the most terrible thing in the world, and, though it doesn't make it any less cruel, crucifixion had become almost a daily punishment for slaves—during the siege of Jerusalem a few years later the Romans were to crucify 500 Jews a day. Our Lord, with his perfect knowledge and self-control would adjust his mind to the physical pain more easily than those who rebel against it. He knew that the hard wood of the cross and the metal of the nails were obeying the laws of their nature and could not help the relentless pressure on the exposed nerves of his hands and feet, and that the nerves too were fulfilling their purpose in protesting to his numbed and tired brain.

What must have hurt him far more were the souls of those mocking, jeering priests, who, even while they were sneering at his helplessness, depended on his love for their very existence. The whole essence, so to speak, of the Passion, its whole meaning, was to make plain to men what had been their response to God's love from the beginning—what it was that Our Lord was asking his Father to forgive.

That is what stares us in the face, as it stared him in the face while he hung on the cross, in the gloating mockery of the materialistic priests, who were proving to everybody that they had been right after all; in the contempt of the worldly-wise Romans shown by the sham coronation and the placard above his head: "This is Jesus, the King of the Jews"; in the complete indifference of the vast crowds who only a few days before had acclaimed him as their king. The gospels make it quite clear that there was no great sympathetic crowd there: crowds did indeed go past on their way to the "more important" sacrifice in the Temple, but only a small handful of women stayed to see him die and the bored guards who played dice to decide who should get his clothes when at last he did die. There stood revealed the whole history of the human race, and it is among them that we must look for ourselves.

"And they that passed by blasphemed him, wagging their heads... and the people stood beholding, and the rulers, with them, derided him, saying: He saved others. Let him save himself, if he be the Christ, the chosen of God. And the soldiers also mocked him, coming to him and offering him vinegar, and saying: If thou be the king of the Jews, save thyself".

And yet even that scene had been prophesied in every detail a thousand years before in that psalm of King David, which, even now—in words that have been so misunderstood—Our Lord began to try and recite:

"My God, my God, why hast thou forsaken me?... I am become the reproach of men and the outcast of the people. All they that saw me have laughed me to scorn. They have spoken with their lips and wagged their heads, saying: 'He hoped in the Lord, let Him deliver him: let Him save him, seeing He delighted in him'.... I am poured out, like water; my strength is dried up, and my tongue has cleaved to my mouth. They have dug my hands and my feet: they have numbered all my bones. They have looked and stared upon me. They have divided my garments among them, and upon my vesture they have cast lots".

He was not able to finish it, as his strength was ebbing away fast. But he managed to gather enough strength for his next words: "Consummatum est". "It has been fulfilled".

And so he had finished the work which his Father had given him to do. Like the mute scapegoat, burdened with the sins of men and left to die outside the city walls, the true Lamb of God, the true reflection of his infinite love and pity, had come and taken away the sins of the whole world.

And he would, surely, want us to end with those words with which I began: "He was offered, because it was his own will". For that, surely, is why the two disciples on the road to Emmaus felt their hearts burning within them, when he said to them: "O foolish, and slow of heart to believe in all things which the prophets have spoken. Ought not Christ to have suffered these things, and so to enter into his glory? And beginning at Moses and all the prophets he expounded to them in all the scriptures the things that were concerning him".

And our repaying that love will be our greatest joy when we come to our heavenly home, where that "crowd which no man can number" pours out its adoration and gratitude to "the Lamb that was slain", and who "hast redeemed us to God in thy blood out of every tribe and tongue and people and nation".

AFTERWORD

by James P. MacGuire

I FIRST MET FATHER JULIAN STEAD, TO WHOM
these extraordinary letters and sermons by Father Julian Stonor
were entrusted by the estate of Noreen Stonor Drexel, in the Fall
of 1965, when my father took me to the then Portsmouth Priory
for my entrance interview. Father Julian was then director of
admissions in addition to his other teaching responsibilities (he
also ran the rifle club, as I recall, which has for perhaps prudential
reasons not survived into the twenty-first century). We toured
the campus from the original Manor House of the old George
Gardner Hall estate, designed by Richard Upjohn in the 1850s,
past the massive neo-Gothic brick of Saint Benet's House designed
by Maginnis and Walsh as a prototype for the entire campus (a
scheme happily derailed by the Depression), to the ethereal and
sublime mid-twentieth century modernist church, monastery, and
dining hall complex designed in redwood and fieldstone by Pietro
Belluschi. Father Julian commented on all these architectural styles
knowledgeably and was a congenial guide to my Dad (a fellow
Old Boy), and me.

When I entered the school in September of 1966 I was assigned
to Father Julian's section of Latin A. "The only thing more bor-
ing than taking Latin I is teaching Latin I," he later remarked. I
rather doubt I increased his pleasure in the task by jumping out
a classroom window in the old Barn with my friend Michael Gay
one especially hot and airless September morning. Father Julian's
comment on my report card at the end of that term was (truly,
alas), "Only the occasional yawn would reassure me he had not
fallen asleep altogether." Years later, when I recounted this to the
lay headmaster in the first decade of the twenty-first century, Dr
James DeVecchi grew visibly nervous and said, "We don't let them
write comments like that anymore." A pity!

Since Father Julian Stead, in order not to deflect attention from
Father Julian Stonor, was so reticent about his own biography in
his introduction to this book, let me add a few details gleaned
from the afterword to his book of poems, *There Shines Forth Christ.*

"To start at the beginning: on November 20, 1926, the wife of the chaplain of Worcester College, Oxford, left a performance of *No, No, Nanette* at the New Theatre ... and gave birth to me at a nursing home on Walton Street, opposite Worcester.... My early childhood was spent around Worcester College, where my father (William Force Stead, a poet whose work W. B. Yeats included in *Oxford Book of Modern Verse*) was a fellow; but at Blackfriars on Saint Giles, in August of 1933, he and I were received into the Roman Catholic Church by the Dominican Father Bede Jarrett. In April 1952 I was ordained to the Catholic priesthood in the same Dominican church while studying theology at Blackfriars as a member of Saint Benet's Hall. In between Saint Giles and Walton Street is 'The Studio', a mews flat on Pusey Lane, where Jean and Sheldon Vanauken lived that year I was studying at Blackfriars, and my friendship with them and the circle of Christians who used to meet in 'The Studio' made a mark on my subsequent life."

(This included lifelong friendships with Tom Howard, Peter Kreeft and other Catholic intellectuals.)

" ... To return to my own life: the only place which has not triggered any poetry in me is the place where I spent my happiest years, Worth Priory (now an Abbey) in Sussex. I went to school there from the age of 8 to 12. It was an earthly paradise for me."

It was at Worth that the then Peter Stead met Father Julian Stonor, from whom he eventually took his name in religion. What higher compliment could one pay?

"I have not intended to put myself on display, but to share with my fellow creatures what may be either an echo or a stimulus of their own feelings for God, for man, and for God's created world of nature."

Gregory Wolfe, editor of *IMAGE* magazine, praised Father Julian Stead for his poetry.

> When I came to read *There Shines Forth Christ*, instead of the somewhat larger-than-life figure I expected, I found a man—a literate and devout man, to be sure, but one troubled by the same daily struggle to be open to God's love and call to holiness that any Christian experiences. Moreover, I found a poet who had mastered his craft and who was able to write of his spiritual life directly, with simplicity and fervor.

"Earth has its heaven, its home," Dom Julian's poem "Maryland" begins, and some of his most moving poems derive from places he has lived or studied in. Raised in England, with youthful years in Kentucky and Maryland, study in Rome, and half a lifetime in the monastery of Portsmouth Abbey in Rhode Island, the poet has found more than one heaven on earth. His poems of place are also Christian poems because he sees both the *createdness* of nature, and the stamp of human character on long-hallowed places. Again, is it a coincidence that the poet should be a Benedictine monk with a vow of stability?

Here is a poem of Father Julian Stead's:

SEA MOON

The moon is the landlord of the night
His face impassive and his movement unharried, unhurried
He watches men die and marry and be born
He looks down through lowered eyelids
And watches what he does not see
How can he hear the moth gasping in the ocean?
Lift up your voice and cry
He cannot hear
Your voice cannot fill the sea and sky
Go down
The way down is the way upward
Darkness down, never to see
The unfeeling starlight
But the sweet salt dark and the brightness
Of the deep height.

It is clear from Father Stonor's letters to Noreen Drexel that they and Father Julian Stead all shared a deep bond with the outdoors, nature, and the nature of Creation. In particular, all three shared a love for horses and riding. Father Stonor writes to Noreen about meeting "keepers and the woodmen" they all knew so well while riding through the Stonor lands, and Father Julian Stead has vivid memories of seeing Billy Barton, a legendary winner of the Hunt Cup in his Maryland youth.

Father Julian Stead and I stayed in touch after my graduation from Portsmouth, and in the mid-1980s, while working at Macmillan, I asked him for advice on researching English recusants, those families who had remained staunchly Catholic at great cost after the Reformation. He suggested I write Lord Camoys of Stonor Park, who in turn introduced me to his sister Georgina, the redoubtable archivist and historian. Another stroke of good fortune came when my Portsmouth classmate and dear friend Christopher Buckley, whose marriage Father Julian had blessed in Saint Matthew's Cathedral in Washington the previous year, asked if he could collaborate on the project. The following summer, 1986, we went off to London to begin our research on a play about Queen Elizabeth I and the martyred Jesuit, Saint Edmund Campion.

JOURNEYS WITH GEORGINA

With Georgina as our guide to what they would have looked like in the sixteenth century, we walked the old London streets, Tower Hill, Leadenhall, and Bank. We visited venerable churches like Saint Olav's, where Pepys worshipped, and All Hallow on Tower Hill. The Tower itself looked so peaceful on a summer day, but inside the walls it was anything but. "Little Ease" was a hideous crack in the wall where Campion was kept four days and three nights, neither able to sit or to stand upright; the Rat Hole was a horrific chamber where one stood surrounded by a rising Thames; the Gibbet was a metal frame in which the executed body was placed and hung; and the Rack, cruelest of all English instruments of torture, where Campion was stretched four inches, claimed in tourist literature to have been "taken from ships of the Spanish Armada."

Saint Henry Walpole S. J. scratched his name elegantly into the Tower wall and then, after being racked, did it a second time in a crippled hand. He had been present at Campion's execution and stained by Campion's blood. He determined then to convert, give up his law practice, and become a priest. Robert Southwell S. J. the poet, was also there and did the same. Such was Campion's charisma.

Later that morning, we went to Tyburn, the place of execution, near Marble Arch, awash in sun and filled with secretaries tanning on their lunch breaks beside the reflecting pool.

Rain, rain on Tyburn tree,
Red rain a-falling;
Dew, dew on Tyburn tree,
And the swart bird a-calling.
  (Francis Thompson, "Ode to the English Martyrs")

Then we were off to Hampton Court, home of Cardinal Wolsey, the proud prelate, whose gift of it to Henry VIII did not long delay his descent after he failed to win papal permission for the divorce. We returned to Bayswater and sat in Alisdair Horne's exquisite garden in Saint Petersburg Road. That evening we ate at Chelsea Wharf with its lovely view of the Thames, just down the road from the house of Saint Thomas More.

The next day we saw Tudor faces at the National Portrait Gallery, all known to Campion, such as Walsingham, the cruelest and most villainous. Then we went off to Hatfield House, home of the Cecils, prominent in the realm for 400 years.

And on to Oxford and the Anglican Church of Saint Mary the Virgin where Campion would have preached had he not converted and where he later left the *Decem Rationes* (the *Ten Reasons for Being a Catholic*, which he had printed on the illegal press at Stonor Park, hidden behind the stair case in a hole called "Mount Pleasant"). New College, with its medieval road leading to it, cloistered quad, and magnificent chapel with its touching war memorial, sent chills up one's spine.

STONOR

That afternoon we drove to Stonor through the old lands, the Weld estate, and what is left, in the distance from a roadside hill, of Lyford Grange, where Campion was captured after a three-day search. Then we drove into Stonor Park itself, a vast pile with fallow deer gathered under a tree. At one point the Stonor family holdings had extended into ten counties.

Georgina introduced us to Derek, the caretaker, and Alina, Georgina's niece who was preparing to read history at Oxford. She was small and slim, blonde with the dark Stonor eyes and a low voice. "She is very argumentative" said her aunt with a twinkling eye and feigned disapproval. Alina then introduced us to her two guests, one the American girl who coxed the Harvard team at

Henley and the other young Di Lampedusa, visiting from Italy.

In the 1950s Evelyn Waugh wrote: "The origins of the house are lost among the speculations of archaeologists. Certainly in 1349 when Sir John de Stonore was granted a royal license to alienate in mortmain provision for six chaplains, the chapel was an ancient foundation. Its massive flint walls are supported by a 'pudding-stone' and from this it is plausibly argued that the site was a place of pagan worship and that a mission station was established there before the age of St. Augustine. The absence of any diocesan record of its consecration suggests very great antiquity."

And in his book *Stonor*, Father Julian Stonor points to evidence of a Celtic Christianity in the Chilterns as early as the second century, long pre-dating the Saxon invasion.

In the chapel are arresting Stations of the Cross, masterpieces of piety, carved on packing crates by a Polish prisoner of war in WWII and given by Graham Greene.

We walked up toward the altar and knelt to pray. Mass has been said in this holy place continuously since the sixth century, and throughout the worst of the Penal Times.

Lady Cecily Stonor to the Justices at Oxford:

> I was born in such a time when Holy Mass was in great reverence ... now in this time it pleaseth the State to question them, as they now do me, who continue in this Catholic profession.... I hold me still that wherein I was born and bred, and find nothing taught in it but great virtue and sanctity and so by the grace of God I will live and die in it.

I prayed, that day, for Father Julian Stead and the cure for the crippling depression that had led him to Affirmation House in Massachusetts for a year, yet another bond he shared with Father Julian Stonor.

Georgina told us about Father Julian Stonor that day and his heroism at Dunkirk as chaplain to the Irish Guards, celebrating Mass upon the beach during the retreat. When, after D-Day, he was refused permission to join his men in Europe because of his poor health, he made a pilgrimage to Skellig Patrick in Ireland where he prayed penitentially for them for four weeks. His soldiers and their sons and daughters still come to the house to ask for him and to pray. When I had written Father Julian Stead about our impending visit he responded, "And bury my heart at Stonor," quoting his old teacher. When I mentioned this to Georgina, she looked startled, then said quietly, "He must have known him very well." When I recounted that exchange to Father Julian Stead a year or two later, he simply said, "Intimately."

We toured the house, saw the mixed American and English furnishing, marveled at the carpentry that fashioned the invisible priest holes, false chimneys, and hidden passages, the immense roof that dates to the tenth century, and realized why priest searches by the Crown could take up to ten days. Then we were treated to tea, laughing at Georgina's stories of Graham Greene putting the Stonor children in his novels surreptitiously and drinking too much port with the old Camoys, of Benjamin Britten's visits, of Waugh's visits, and of the tragedy of the old Lord, who began wearing a parachute jacket to the House of Lords and slowly drank himself away. Happily, the house was saved.

Then back to London, Thursday lunch at the Garrick with Alisdair Horne, Richard Olivier holding forth at his table, and, in the evening, *The Mysteries* at the Lyceum, a thrilling contemporary recreation of medieval folk drama. "God" was particularly charming, like a Lancashire Eric Hoffer.

FATHER JULIAN STEAD AND NOREEN STONOR DREXEL

Father Julian Stead came to Portsmouth, Rhode Island, first as a student and later as a monk, and thereby remained in occasional—but latterly more frequent—touch with the favorite cousin of his old teacher, Father Julian Stonor: Noreen Stonor Drexel. She was living eight miles away, in Newport.

Noreen Drexel died peacefully on November 6, 2012 after suffering a stroke, just ten days after celebrating her ninetieth birthday, surrounded by family and friends. Mrs. Drexel was the *doyenne* of Newport, just as she had been a leading lady until recent years in New York and Palm Beach.

Born the Honorable Noreen Stonor in Henley-on-Thames in England, Mrs. Drexel was the youngest daughter of Ralph Stonor, Fifth Baron Camoys of Stonor Park in Oxfordshire, and Lady Camoys, the former Mildred Sherman, a daughter of prominent New York banker William Watts Sherman. On her mother's side,

Mildred was a descendent of Rhode Island's founder, Roger Williams, and of Nicholas Brown, the founder of Brown University. She brought Noreen, then a teenager, to Newport, Rhode Island on the eve of World War II.

None of this exalted background prevented Noreen, as she preferred to be called, from undertaking a lifetime of good works. She was a volunteer in three wars—World War II, Korea, and Vietnam—and a tireless advocate, mainly through the Red Cross, of maternal and child well-being and mental health. She was hands on—a nurse's aide at the Newport Naval Hospital, working on blood drives, helping in the emergency room and on the hospital wards, even driving an ambulance! And all of this was done with the utmost loving, personal kindness. She opened her charming Victorian house on Bellevue Avenue to the great and not-so-great. Every year, after presiding over the summer season, she had a reception for the many charities she supported. She was the 2011 honoree of the Newport Hospital Gala. The hospital's Noreen Stonor Drexel Birthing Center welcomes newborn children to Newport, a city that Mrs. Drexel, through her chairmanship of the Aletta Morris McBean Charitable trust and other philanthropies, had done so much to improve.

Noreen married John R. Drexel III, a kinsman of Mother Katherine Drexel and a descendant of the founder of Philadelphia's Drexel University, in 1941. They had three children, Pamela, Nick, and Nonie, and seven grandsons.

We first became friends in 1987 when Christopher Buckley's and my play, *Campion*, premiered at the Williamstown Theatre Festival. Noreen and John Drexel made the long trip from Newport up to the Berkshires to see it, possibly the only time in that Bohemian setting that a couple attended a performance in evening clothes!

In more recent years my sons, Pierce and Rhoads, and Noreen's grandsons (Nonie's boys)—Liam, Fergus, Aidan and Finnian O'Farrell—became schoolmates and close friends at Portsmouth, and Noreen was their biggest booster at games and other school functions.

Her funeral at Saint John the Evangelist Church in Newport on November 10, 2012, was presided over by the Episcopal Bishop of Rhode Island. A large reception was held afterward at the Pell Center at Salve Regina University, which Noreen did so much to develop and now boasts both Stonor and Drexel Halls.

"I'm a frustrated nurse!" Noreen liked to exclaim. No one ever gave more kindly or more lovingly than Noreen, and her example will be her greatest legacy.

There is a compelling homecoming with which to close this story.

The young Noreen Stonor had received a papal dispensation to marry the socially prominent Philadelphian John Drexel in his Episcopal Church, and she carried out her wifely duties faithful to her vows. But after Mr Drexel's death her own ancestral faith still tugged upon her heart, and who was able to intercede that she might be able to resume Catholic worship and receive the true Body and Blood of Christ, but Cousin Julian's student and namesake in religion, Father Julian Stead?

And thereafter, in the last years of her life, she was a regular attendee of the sung Mass on Sundays at Portsmouth Abbey.

After her Newport funeral, Noreen's body was taken to England for a Catholic Mass and burial beside her mother in a village cemetery high in the Chilterns, with a beautiful view of her birthplace, Stonor.

Later, the furniture she and her mother had brought from Stonor when they came to Newport was removed from the Bellevue Avenue house (which later burned down while undergoing renovations by its new owners) and is safely back at Stonor Park once again.

"I think it may have been the best thing I ever did," Father Julian Stead told me of Noreen's re-conversion as we prepared this book for publication. Surely Father Julian Stonor would agree. And may Father Stonor's letters and sermons, passed on by Mrs. Drexel's estate to Father Julian Stead, live on, and inspire renewed interest in Father Stonor and Stonor Park as a place of pilgrimage.

APPENDIX

STONOR PARK,
HENLEY-ON-THAMES.
12th May, 1955.

My dear Julian,

The Archbishop of Birmingham spent last night here, bringing with him the splendid news that Witham & Co., are ready to hand over the wonderful gift of £1,000 from your anonymous benefactor. The Archbishop is most enthusiastic about the restoration of the Chapel, and has approved all that I propose to do. We found him in all ways easy and charming, and I hope this will be the first of many visits. He seems to be very well disposed towards the family, and is perfectly satisfied about the status of the Chapel, and he shares all your feelings about the English Martyrs and wishes to do everything he can to help us make the Chapel beautiful and there is no doubt that he looks upon it as a Shrine. This is the first time in my memory that a really happy relationship has existed between the Arch-diocese and ourselves, and I am certain it is in great measure due to your prayers and efforts.

-We were-

We were all a bit sad at not hearing from you at Easter, and I am worried to learn indirectly that you are looking far from well and obviously not happy teaching small boys. I have a feeling, however, that things may be going to turn out better for you, and I pray that this will indeed be the case. This is not from anything that the Archbishop said and I can only tell you that some of your old friends are very worried about you. Do try and find time to let me know how you are and do also try and take some care of your health.

Please pass on to whoever it is our most grateful thanks for such kindness and generosity. I would of course like to make some record in the Chapel of the person concerned, so that he or she can be remembered in our prayers and commemorated as the person mainly responsible for the restoration.

With love from us all.

Yours affectionately,

Stonor.

COPY

Barn Cottage,
Maidensgrove,
Henley-on-Thames.

February 15th 1963.

My dear Sherman and Jeanne,

We were so touched by your thoughtfulness in ringing
up Tuesday morning - alas, to give us the dreaded news. We
feel for you both, and for all your family, so very much. As
Ronnie said, "It is as if a light has gone out and the world's
a poorer place for his leaving it." But though that's true,
and one feels his loss so acutely, as if the world will never
be quite the same again, one should really say, "But how much
richer the world is for his living in it," for the measure of
our loss is only the measure of the richness he gave to each of
the countless hundreds of people with whom he came into contact
wherever he went.

Julian's presence, even in physical absence, radiated
hope, courage, joy, enthusiasm, eternal youth, boundless energy,
gentleness, purity, faith, light and an abundance of all-
embracing love. He seemed to have wings, and to give wings to o
others; to move among all men with grace and *in* grace, so that
the most leaden hearts were touched by it and responded to that
undefinable, gossamer quality, in the same way that even the
wildest of wild birds came, unafraid, to his hands.

I think the secret is in the last four lines of his
lovely poem, 'The Apostle':
"I know, now that I never see
The print of his feet in the dust,
That in every man for ever
I meet the son of God."
He saw the divinity in all of us, and the layers of swaddling
clothes with which we cover it did not matter to him. To him,
they were transparencies, to be gently unwrapped with infinite
patience, understanding and love.

One doesn't want to question God's wisdom, but his
span was so short. It seems only the other day that I was out
for a walk at South Ascot and saw a little boy ahead of me on
the road, and my Nanny said, "There's the little Stonor boy. D
Doesn't he look pale." Well, he has always been pale - and
always ahead of me on the road. And now ahead of us all, and in
the warm sunshine of God's love. He will pray for us.

God bless you both,
Yours,

Peggy.

ACKNOWLEDGMENTS

This book could not have been completed without the help of Dr Timothy Flanigan, Jeanne Perrotti and the oblates of Portsmouth Abbey, Red Cummings (Portsmouth Abbey 1963), Susanne Reid, and Cynthia Nebergall. We are deeply indebted to Dr Peter Kreeft and Nonie Drexel for their preface and foreword. Finally, Father Julian Stead's patience, persistence, and devotion to the memory of Father Julian Stonor and Noreen Stonor Drexel in bringing this book to fruition should be saluted. *Ad multos annos!*

CPSIA information can be obtained
at www.ICGtesting.com
Printed in the USA
BVHW030844160223
658549BV00025B/180/J